The Wings *of* Destiny

The Wings *of* Destiny

Molly Odegard Nikolic

THE WINGS OF DESTINY

This book is written to provide information and motivation to readers. Its purpose is not to render any type of psychological, legal, or professional advice of any kind. The content is the sole opinion and expression of the author, and not necessarily that of the publisher.

Copyright © 2019 by Molly Odegard Nikolic

All rights reserved. No part of this book may be reproduced, transmitted, or distributed in any form by any means, including, but not limited to, recording, photocopying, or taking screenshots of parts of the book, without prior written permission from the author or the publisher. Brief quotations for noncommercial purposes, such as book reviews, permitted by Fair Use of the U.S. Copyright Law, are allowed without written permissions, as long as such quotations do not cause damage to the book's commercial value. For permissions, write to the publisher, whose address is stated below.

Printed in the United States of America.

ISBN   978-1-64552-144-0   (Paperback)
ISBN   978-1-64552-145-7   (Digital)

Lettra Press books may be ordered through booksellers or by contacting:

Lettra Press LLC
30 N Gould St. Ste N
Sheridan, WY 82801, USA
3035861431 | info@lettrapress.com
www.lettrapress.com

Acknowledgements

Molly Odegard Nikolic, thanks:

Dejan Nikolic, for his plot suggestions, encouragement and help;

Sarah Whelan Blake, for her typing, knowledge of theater and wonderful friendship;

Dr. Fred W. Blancke, for his super support, friendship, willingness to listen to me read the text and his excellent advice;

Dr. Nenad Obradovic, for his private remembrances of what happened to him during the war;

Bob J. Joha, for sharing his difficult remembrances of the war;

Kendra Karaklajic, for her knowledge of publishing, lovely friendship and encouragement;

Barbara L. Willets, for her memories of Goff and her support.

Chapter 1

Being a professional actress is not an easy career, but when you've been bitten by the acting bug, you're doomed. Why do I say doomed? Because it can take away so much of what normal life is about. I'm talking about the ordinary things in life, like a stable married life with children and a home. I don't know if I was born with the acting bug or did it come later to me, but it certainly ruled the first part of my life. I look at the world of theater and film—oh, I guess they say movies now—and I see the same thing happening. What's it all for? For fame and money, that's what. It's a purely selfish endeavor. In my early days, they hadn't discovered the idea of genetic forces leading people into things unknown. I do understand that Freud played with this field, but regular people didn't know about it. We all just did what we did. Often people are looked at because of preconceived notions or what was an established family tradition. You swam alone, going into uncharted waters of your own desire and making. Well, that's what I did. Am I sorry? Partially. I left my first husband for it, and I gave up my one and only child.

St. Paul, Minnesota, back in 1914, was an active place filled with all kinds of people all working to create prosperous lives for themselves. The Great War had just begun, but most of us were unaware of it and what it was doing to Europe. We were all happily discovering the many things life had to offer. For me, I discovered Goff Leveroos. Oh, he was something: young and handsome with big, sexy blue eyes and a manner about him that certainly melted my heart—and could he dance, especially to his favorite song, "After the Ball."

My mother, Gloria Taylor, had been in theater long before I discovered and loved it. Mother was a fabulous actress. She could make an audience laugh or cry just by walking onstage—it was amazing. One night she brought me to one of her shows as a replacement for a little girl whose mother wouldn't let her do the show anymore. All I had to do was walk into the scene and start crying when I hear that my toy dog was lost and couldn't be found anywhere. It was so easy, and I was good—at least everyone said so. I've been doing theater ever since and loving every minute of it.

Later I also fell in love with doing film. The big problem with film is that it's a time waster. You start a scene and because something happens—the lights break down or the wind comes up or it starts raining or snowing—everything has to stop and the whole thing has to be done over. If the lights break down in the theater you just ad lib a little and say something like, "Darling, it's getting awfully dark. Would you go and bring some candles or an oil lamp?" That's not the way it works in film.

It was in March of 1917 I gave up everything to become a professional actress. First the theater called, blinding me, and then films. I couldn't resist. Life wasn't easy then. My husband, Goff, was away in the war, and our daughter, Betty Gray, was just a baby.

There was bad blood between Goff's family and us, especially toward me, the actress, and, I thought, toward Betty Gray too. Living together was sometimes a nightmare. My mother-in-law Sarah strongly disapproved that her son married an actress, and I didn't want her raising Betty Gray and filling her head with terrible things about me, such as I was a low-class actress who ran off and left her. I didn't do that. Betty was always on my mind and in my heart. I love her. One day, after again hearing words from Sarah about something she disapproved of, I left the house to get away from her. As I walked out the apartment building's entrance door, I met our neighbor Harriet Oates, who was heading out to the market. Harriet was a nice but ordinary lady. As we walked she began to tell me of the older, wealthy couple she worked for, Frank and Mollie Carey, who desperately had wanted a baby but couldn't conceive. She went on and on about how kind they were and what wonderful parents they would be. I couldn't work in New York as an actress if I didn't have a place for Betty. I needed New York; I also needed a place for Betty. I really didn't want to leave her with my mother-in-law Sarah. I couldn't stand the thought of Sarah putting terrible thoughts against me into Betty's sweet head, which she would have done for sure. You're probably wondering about Goff; he didn't know. I didn't tell him of my plans nor did I get the chance. I know, I know—it was just plain selfish. So begins the confessions and story of an actress.

By mid-March, a fairly thick blanket of snow still covered the city, remarkably still sparkling just as it did when a vicious blizzard fell two months ago. Forty-five-year-old Mollie Carey looked lovingly down at the baby girl sleeping in her crib. She gently rocked the dark-brown wicker crib, wondering about the child sleeping so peacefully. "Who are you? Who are your people? Why did your real mother leave you? She never gave herself the chance to be a mother to you. I'm sure she wanted to be. Poor dear. Life is strange. I'll do everything in my power to make you happy, to protect you and care for you. You're mine now."

An hour later, little five-month-old Betty Gray was up from her nap. She sat playing on a blanket Mollie had put down on the living room floor, near the window of their house in Minneapolis. A gentle breeze, blowing from the furnace, mussed the child's natural, slightly curled brown hair, blowing it across her face. She brushed it with her hand, trying to get it out of her eyes as best she could. A moment later she laughed as she gently threw one of her small wooden alphabet blocks out onto the rug while securely hugging her new toy dog with the other hand.

Six months earlier, beautiful blue skies filled with big, lazy, fluffy clouds gave the days a sense of gentleness. Mollie Carey was resting. She'd been ill recently; both her body and her heart had been hurt when she'd lost, for the fifth time, a child—another son was delivered stillborn. This son, Thomas Eugene Carey, had come three months too soon. He was buried beside his brothers before he even had a chance to breathe or live. As with the other four babies, Mollie and Frank had given him a name, an identity. He wasn't a nothing. He was a somebody—their son.

Hearing any baby laugh or gurgle at that time brought a huge hard lump to Mollie's throat, the kind that doesn't let you cry but sticks there, like a knife, not letting one speak.

My son, my darling little boy, my last hope, why were you taken from me? Why is God punishing me? she thought, again feeling that horrid lump trying to form in her throat. She hadn't wept for several days about this, but now to just think of the child again brought it all back. At age forty-five, Thomas had been Mollie's last chance for a child.

Chapter 2

Harriet Oates, housekeeper to the Careys, stood outside on the porch, looking at the snow as she knocked on the heavy, clear, etched-glass wooden-framed door. She was half an hour early. The streetcar, for some reason, had only six people this morning and only four stops instead of the usual ten or more. Arriving earlier than expected, Harriet was happy to start the day ahead of schedule. Maybe she'd have time to surprise Mrs. Carey by polishing some of the dining room silver today with the extra time, plus she had news.

She knocked again with the ball-shaped door knocker, harder and stronger this second time. It took Mollie a moment to realize the noise she heard wasn't some simple distraction from the street but her own door. Slowly she rose from the couch, going over to see about the noise.

"Oh, top o' the morning to you," Mrs. Oakes, with her singing Irish brogue, greeted Mollie as she came in.

"And the same to you. You're early today."

"Aye, there were very few riders today, practically had the streetcar to myself. Can I be getten you your tea?" the slightly heavyset woman with green eyes asked as she looked at Mrs. Carey. "Glory be. You've been cryin' again."

Mollie nodded. She seemed to cry all the time. There didn't need to be a reason; the tears just came.

"There, there, Mrs. Carey. You come over here and sit yourself down. I'll have your tea ready faster than a tinker's damn." Harriet Oakes liked Mollie Carey very much. She'd always been extremely fair and more than kind to the lady from Ireland, giving her extra days off when needed and paying her extra, just because she wanted to. They had become friends—not to the point of Mollie Carey ever inviting Harriet and her second husband Billy to dinner, but friends in the way that they seemed to almost know when something was wrong or when something good was happening with each other.

"Thank you," she said quietly, feeling Mrs. Oates's arm gently escorting her back to the dark royal-blue velvet couch. The couch had been a wedding gift from Frank's aunt Florence and uncle Paul. She loved the rich color and how comfortable it was. "Would you make me a slice of toast too, please?"

"Of course, being my pleasure." At that she was off to the kitchen.

Harriet Oates couldn't help but have empathy for Mrs. Carey. It took a little less than fifteen minutes to get the kettle to boil, the tea made, and the toast prepared. Harriet poured the tea in one of the Royal Doulton cups Mollie and Frank had bought when they arrived to Minneapolis and poured one for herself. She then loaded a large, highly etched silver tray with the teapot, cup and saucer, plate, and the toast rack, adding, before she went out the kitchen door, a pot of strawberry jam and a plate with butter and the silverware.

When she got back she saw for the first time how red Mollie's eyes were. The lady didn't look tired, but her eyes had an unmistakable look of sadness, which cast an expression on Mrs. Carey's face, making her look different, older, and vulnerable. Harriet Oates's heart again went out to her employer. Harriet couldn't help but have empathy for Mrs. Carey. The woman had suffered so much over the loss of her child. Harriet also knew this pain, having lost her firstborn too. There had been a number of nights when the wee one would fill Harriet's dreams, calling out, "Mama," only to dissipate as Harriet would wake up, leaving her feeling as though she'd been a victim of theft. They'd been together for nearly three years, and in all that time she'd never seen Mrs. Carey any way in a depressed mood. It was in fact quite the opposite. Entertaining was the normal routine; everyone from her book club and the Women's League to her husband's important business and political friends had brought happy business to the house. Now little Thomas, as Harriet liked to call him, had left a gray mantle shrouding the place. She could clearly see how the loss of this little boy had brought a change to Mrs. Carey. Now, as of last night, she had some news that might brighten the dampened spirits of the lady with pretty blue eyes in the living room.

"Mrs. Carey I'd be likin' to talk to you."

"Yes, Mrs. Oates, what is it?" Mollie said, sipping the Irish breakfast tea Harriet had made. "The tea is so pleasant today."

"Thank you, ma'am." She paused watching Mrs. Carey sip the tea. "I know how very sad you've been since we lost little Thomas, but I want to tell you that my neighbor, across the hall from me, Helen Leveroos, brought over her little girl and a big package with 'Betty's things' written on it two days ago, and I'm wondering about her not comin' for her," she said, watching Mrs. Carey enjoy the tea.

"That's interesting. Why?" Mollie asked, smelling the tea and wondering why Harriet was telling her this. She took another sip of the lovely hot brew.

"I'm just wondering that she never came to get the baby."

"That's strange. Who is this woman? Do you know her?"

"Yes, somewhat. Her name is Helen Leveroos. She's a nice lady and such a pretty woman, and I thought a good mother, but a stage actress," Harriet said, lowering her voice as though she'd said a bad word. "They're different, you know. But she always had Betty dressed in the sweetest little dresses and the cutest bonnets. They were so cute together."

"Where is the baby's father?" Mollie asked, simply wanting to know. "She once told me, briefly, her husband was off on a warship someplace in the Atlantic fighting this awful war, but she mostly talked about the theater and the shows she'd been in. It was all very interesting. She really loved the theater and everything about it. I was surprised at the time. She didn't talk much about her baby, her husband, or the war. Theater was the topic. It seemed to be the most important part of her life. She went on to say her mother had been a big name in our local theater world. At the end of a performance one night, she died onstage of a heart attack. It really scared the audience, not to mention the actors and crew. Helen just followed in her mother's step. I saw her twice, and I think she was better than her mother. She really should be in the movies."

"My, my," Mollie said. She'd never heard or thought about actresses before.

"Last night my friend Lillian stopped by to tell me about the show Mrs. Leveroos was in. She was very disappointed Helen Leveroos didn't appear on stage.

"That's strange. I'm glad you've got the baby. Can I help in any way?" Mollie's natural tendencies made her ask.

"Well, that's a good question," Harriet said, admiring her handiwork of the freshly washed and ironed curtains on the windows.

"Who's watching the child now?" Mollie wanted to know.

"She's with me for the moment, but I can't keep her." She paused and then added, "Gee, she's awfully cute. The sweetest wee little darlin' I've ever seen." Harriet looked at Mollie's expression, hoping she'd heard that something, a slight hint coming from her voice, asking for help. The reality was the child couldn't stay with her, but Mrs. Carey was another story, and her loss was fresh, but maybe she wouldn't want to take the child, or maybe she would. It was only until Mrs. Leveroos came back. Harriet crossed her fingers for the latter.

"No, I mean where is the baby at this moment?" Mollie asked, falling into Harriet's plight. Something inside just seemed to push her. Mollie had always been the one the family called on when things weren't right; she instinctively seemed to know what needed doing.

"She's at my place. Lettie Brown, from next door, has the day off from her job at Dayton's, so I asked her to take care of the baby until I get back. Mrs. Leveroos loves that little girl. I'm surprised she hasn't come back for the little one."

"My goodness. I can't believe all of this. Oh, I do believe you. It just seems so strange. My goodness, what modern times have brought."

"Poor little darlin'. Cute as a bug's ear. Tomorrow I'll be having a problem though. You see Mrs. Brown works, so I don't know what I'll be doin' with the baby. Can I bring her? Would it be too much trouble?" Harriet asked, praying Mrs. Carey would say yes.

All of a sudden her look changed. One of excitement came across Mollie's face. Her blue eyes sparkled as she began to smile. "I have a better idea. Let's go and bring her back here," she said. An excitement filled the air, passing itself off onto Harriet, who was truly surprised by the sudden suggestion.

"Are you meaning now?" Harriet asked.

"Yes. No time like the present," Mollie said. Harriet quickly finished her tea as Mollie just left hers, heading upstairs to get her wrap, hat, pocketbook, and the keys to their new electric car. Frank had bought it just for her, wanting her to learn to drive and become a part of modern society. He was very impressed that his wife of twenty-five years, after only four driving lessons, which he had given her, could drive the short machine with tall windows so well.

"Well, all right. It will free Mrs. Brown greatly. But what about my work?" Harriet asked.

"Right now this is your work," Mollie said, opening the door of the dark forest-green car. She truly liked this machine—it was fun—but she still didn't trust it completely, mainly when it went over twenty-five miles an hour; nothing should go faster than a horse, particularly in town.

When they'd gotten in, Mollie pushed the starter switch, pulled up the brake, and put the car in gear. Slowly they started, quietly; almost like a ghost, the car went down the street. Mrs. Oates was in awe—first, because a woman, her employer, drove and, secondly, everything about the car itself was so magnificent. It was much more luxurious than her own house and the ride was so smooth. She'd ridden in one other car and the bus, but the noise and dust was awful. This green electric car, named Electra by Mrs. Carey, was a modern marvel. Harriet was astonished it only took ten minutes to get to her house; the bus took double that time. Oh, Mrs. Carey was so lucky, and she was, too, for getting to ride in such a fine machine.

As the car slowly came toward Harriet's house, Mrs. Brown, holding the baby girl in her arms, looked at the car through the window as it came down the street. She carefully watched as the newfangled car stopped in front of the house.

"Glory be! Would you look at that, little one. Who would be coming here? I can't imagine Mrs. Oates knows anyone with an automobile—it is an automobile, I think," Mrs. Brown said, continuing to watch. Her mouth dropped open when she saw Mrs. Carey and Harriet get out.

"My, my. We'd better open the door to them," Lettie Brown, wife of the city's most famous hunting dog breeder, Alton Brown, said to the little girl.

Mollie and Harriet came up the walkway to an open door. In the threshold stood the woman and the baby, both watching and smiling as they came toward them.

"Mrs. Carey, this is Mrs. Lettie Brown. Shall we go in?"

Mollie was glad to go in, as the sun was very bright and a little hard on her eyes that day. Seeing the child with the big blue eyes looking directly at her, she was immediately smitten. Just as Harriet had said, she was so sweet and pretty, more so than any other child she'd seen, almost like one of Raphael's cherubs, whose hovering presence sweetly adores and protects the Christ child.

"Is this the child whose mother didn't come to get her?" Mollie slowly asked, continuing to look at the beautiful little girl.

"Yes, poor thing," Mrs. Brown said as she handed her over to Harriet. Harriet took the baby, holding her close to her chest. She was small for her age, Harriet thought, wondering if everything was all right with the little girl.

"Was she a good girl?" Harriet asked, smoothing the child's clothing.

"Yes, very. When you left we played for a bit then I put her down for a rest. She's just been awake for a few minutes. She'll be wanting a bottle soon, I would think."

"Very good. Thank you ever so much for taking care of her for me."

"It was my pleasure. I'd love to do it again if you need," Mrs. Brown said, stroking Betty's soft hair.

"I'll keep that in mind. Thank you again," Harriet answered, taking Mrs. Brown to the door. "Bye." As she closed the door, Mollie noticed how small Harriet's home was—neat as a pin, but small, almost like a doll's house.

"Mrs. Carey, this is Helen Leveroos's daughter, Betty Gray," Harriet said, turning so Mollie could see Betty's face.

"My, she is cute. You were absolutely right. Look at those big blue eyes looking out, and that nose and sweet mouth. Her hair looks so soft," Mollie gushed, falling deeply in love.

"Yes, she is something. Here, why don't you take her while I get her bottle ready?" Harriet said, handing over the baby to Mollie's waiting arms. The moment the little girl touched the childless woman's breast, her heart opened totally. At the same moment the pull of motherhood, like a bolt of lightning, called again, making her think maybe little Thomas wasn't her last chance. So this is what Harriet wanted, she realized. She could feel the warmth of the little girl's hand on her cheek. Now she wanted it, too, more than life itself. Was this child to be her miracle, a special gift from God after all the pain of losing the other babies? It didn't matter.

"What is going to happen to her? Her father must be notified," Mollie quietly said, fearing the last several words she'd spoken.

"'Tis true. How does one get in touch with someone on a warship fighting the war?" Harriet wondered out loud.

"I don't know, probably through the recruiting office. Frank will know. I'll ask him when he gets home tonight," Mollie said, almost sorry her sense of fair play ruled her reasoning so strongly. She wanted that little girl.

"He'll know, I'm sure. In the meantime, I can't keep her, so I'm asking you to take her while her place is being determined."

"I'd love to take her, but what about the police? Surely they need to be told where she is. I don't want anyone accusing me of stealing her."

"I'll tell Officer O'Connell when we leave. He's usually stationed on the corner just up the road. He directs traffic, but I don't really think they need to know. Nothing criminal is happening," Harriet said.

"That's true. In the meantime we need to feed her. Is the bottle ready yet?" Mollie asked with great anticipation.

"It should be by now. Why don't you bring her into the kitchen?"

With that Mollie brought Betty Gray into the warm kitchen filled with so many modern cooking contraptions it made her wonder why so much equipment was needed.

Harriet went over to the wood stove; slowly she took the warmed bottle out of the pan of hot water, wiped it with a towel, and handed it to Mrs. Carey. They all sat down at the wooden table covered by a good-quality oil cloth. Mollie positioned Betty on her lap and put the nipple bottle to her mouth. She took it instinctively, sucking hard on it and getting all the milk she could. Soon sweet sounds of contentment and pleasure were heard. When it was all consumed, Mollie put Betty on her shoulder, tapping her gently, waiting for a big burp, which came a moment later.

"You handled that like you've fed lots of babies," Harriet said, taking the tea towel that was used as a bib off the baby.

"She was very hungry. Did you notice she drank almost every drop? Do you suppose she needs changing?"

"Probably. Let's take her to the bathroom. I've got some cloths there ready for this situation."

It didn't take long to change and redress the little one, getting her ready for the trip to Mrs. Carey's house. The baby smiled and cooed during the whole process. As Mollie finished dressing her, Harriet decided, just to make sure, to go up to the corner to talk to Officer O'Connell, who at that moment was very busy trying to deal with two car accidents, three very angry men, and debris in the middle of the intersection from the accidents. As she tried to talk to him about the baby, he abruptly told her, "Woman, don't you see we have a serious situation here? Just go on about your business." He turned away from her to try to calm one of the men who, at that moment, was about to kick the other man's car.

"All right," she said, surprised to be talked to in such a tone but glad she didn't have to give any information that might lead the police to take the baby.

Once in the car, Harriet held Betty, propping her up so she could see out as Mrs. Carey drove the silent electric car down the streets of St. Paul and into Minneapolis, arriving at West Lake of the Isles Boulevard. The Carey house was a large, square two-story home. Four bedrooms, a large sitting room, and two bathrooms made up the upstairs. The downstairs had a very large living room and equally large dining room, a library and a sitting room that they used for playing cards, a big modern kitchen, a pantry, and a maids' quarters after the breakfast room, ending the house with a long back hall and a door leading to the basement. This was the floor plan of the extensive house. Frank, nowadays, could afford such things, becoming a rising player in the fast-growing grain market.

Frank Carey was a fairly large man, Irish, blond with blue eyes, and had a keen sense of business, being the first generation born in America, in Duluth in 1875. He was one of five children. Three sisters and a brother, plus himself, gave his mother plenty of reason for her early gray hair. She wore it like some sort of banner, declaring she'd done her best. They were a close family, keeping in touch through letters and visits all the time. Mollie loved the mini vacations they took with their in-laws and her own family from Montana. She also enjoyed the carefree times spent with her brothers and sisters, sitting and talking and just being together. It was a lovely, gentle way of living.

Frank and Mollie had a happy life together. Even though their home was empty of children, life was active and full; but occasionally Frank would catch a glimpse of his wife stroking a picture of a baby in one of her women's magazines. Then there were the times he would hear her crying in bed, late at night, gently whimpering the names of their lost boys. His heart just sank when he'd hear that. It was hard to deal with a woman's crying, but this repeating the names of their dead sons just about killed him, for there was nothing he could do to bring them back. Why did women go through that, he wondered. He'd then gently pull her close and tell her how much he loved her and that maybe they would have a child one day. Then they'd make love, and all would be better for a while.

"Mrs. Oates, would you open the front door while I get Betty out?" Mollie asked as she parked the car in front of the garage. Mrs. Oates took the package that came with the baby and saw a photograph in it. "Here's a picture of Betty with her mother. What shall I do with it?"

"Put the photo in the attic and her other things in the blue room."

"Being my pleasure for sure," Harriet said, getting the key from Mrs. Carey. Placing it in the lock, Harriet was greeted by the wonderful fresh smell of the house. She was proud of that smell; it showed she'd done her job, and very well. In her youth, back in Ireland, she'd been lucky to be taken in for an apprenticeship as a housekeeper at Lady Maude Kilpatrick's estate just outside of Dublin when she was twelve. It was a hard life and she missed her family, but Lady Maude and Lord John were patient and very kind to her, favoring her and Katie, the other girl there, in many things, like taking both of them occasionally on vacations to the sea or giving them two new dresses at Christmas time. They also gave them enough education to get along in the world. Harriet left the Kilpatricks when she married Claude Maille, a baker there in Dublin. They had a sweet but short life together. Claude Maille died six days after their third wedding anniversary when the big brick oven he was taking bread out of exploded.

Four months after her husband's death, both she and Katie found work with a new family, the Nelans and nine months later Gerald Nelan decided they were all immigrating to America. Venturing off into the New World the girls were glad to put the tough times in Ireland behind them.

Harriet seemed to have the luck of the Irish with her when she landed on American shore Katie didn't. A year after they arrived, Katie was killed in a train accident when she and a new boyfriend were on their way to Wisconsin to visit his cousins. Despite the fact the Nelans gave Harriet a home, work, and a salary, the loss of her husband, baby, and best friend brought a dark time; but she was tough, and she could cope. Slowly as life went on, she came to love Minneapolis and the good people there. Its lakes and green views were different than those in Ireland but also wonderful; it became a place she thought of as home. Six years later the Nelans decided to go west to California. They wanted Harriet to go with them, but she didn't want to. She felt California was too dangerous after hearing stories from the butcher Mr. Miller about life in the mountains and of the weather, dry as a bone in the summer and then cold with horrible snow, like at the North Pole, in the winter, not to mention the dangerous wild animals that ran around and about trouble with the Indians. Plus, she was soon going to marry Billy Oates. She thanked them for the offer, helped them pack, and sent them on their way, promising to keep in touch when she got word from them. Two weeks after the Nelans left, Harriet found work with the Careys and a new life with Billy Oates.

"Come on, Betty. Let's go in the house," Mollie said to the little girl as she opened the passenger's side door. Betty smiled as Mollie lifted her up and into her arms. "This is where I live. Maybe you'll live here too one day. Harriet, we need to get the rose room ready for Betty."

"Yes, indeed."

"It's right next to ours. I want to be able to hear her," she said, putting the little girl down on the floor. Betty quietly sat there, looking around the large room. She seemed contented, not crying or whimpering but just sitting there. All of a sudden she fell backward, crying when she lightly hit her head on the floor. Immediately Mollie jumped up, gathering her in her arms, soothing her.

"There, there, it's all right. You just had a little tumble. You're okay. Don't cry, sweetheart," Mollie said, quieting Betty's fears. She gently rubbed the back of her head. Slowly the sobbing stopped. Her big blue-gray eyes were red with crying which distressed Mollie. The child wasn't supposed to be unhappy immediately. "Let's get you a little milk and maybe a cracker, then let's go to see your new room." Hearing the gentleness of the words from the nice lady, Betty Gray began to smile. Everything seemed fine now, but it had given Mollie a terrible scare.

They walked into the kitchen where Mollie got a cracker for the child. She had no idea what babies ate. Betty was about six months old, she thought. Crackers were probably all right and milk for sure was good, but what else? She decided she'd get in touch with a pediatrician tomorrow. She took her back into the living room, put her down on the new rose brocade couch in the corner, and propped her up with a pillow to support to her.

"Mrs. Carey, I can't find the baby crib up here in the attic. I've looked where I thought we'd put it," Harriet called from upstairs after she'd put the photo of Helen and Betty behind the chimney.

"What, Harriet? I can't hear you properly," Mollie called back, getting up to get closer to the stairs.

"I can't find the crib. We need it for the baby's room," she called out. "Oh, it's not in sight? All right. I'm coming." Mollie looked over toward Betty. Seeing she was safely stationed in the corner of the couch, she felt free to go to help Harriet.

Just as Mollie got halfway up the stairs, Frank came in the kitchen door. It was Friday afternoon nothing of importance was happening in the office, so he decided to take the rest of the day off. On the way home he decided he'd take Mollie out for dinner that night, wanting her to feel better, and she did love to go to that little French café on Hennipen Avenue. They didn't go out often, but Mollie deserved a little special attention.

As he walked into the living room, he spotted Betty sitting in the corner of the couch.

"Well, hello. Who are you?" he said, coming closer. She smiled up at him with the most beautiful blue-gray eyes he'd ever seen. "My, my. What have we here?" he said, picking her up. "Mollie! Mollie!" he called out. He put her back down on the couch, took his hat and coat off and put them away in the closet. He came back to sit beside the baby, picking her up and putting her on his lap. She cooed and smiled, looking straight at him. He smiled back, and they smiled at each other until Mollie came.

"Oh, I see you've met. Isn't she wonderful?" his wife said, coming downstairs from the attic after helping Harriet get the crib into the hall. She sat down on the matching chair across from them and looked at her husband.

"Ah, yes, but where does she come from?" he slowly asked, looking at her.

"It's kind of a long story. Harriet told me of her. A few days ago her mother gave her to Harriet to look after, but she didn't come to pick her up. Harriet had to be here today, so she gave her to her neighbor Mrs. Brown to take care of. Well, when Harriet told me of the situation I suggested we go to get the baby and bring her here, so we did."

"Oh," Frank said with a thousand thoughts of what was really supposed to happen to the little girl going through his mind. "Ah, Mollie, you know we can only keep her for a while, until her mother comes back."

"I know, but she's here now until we find out where she belongs. Her father is in the navy, off on a ship, and since her mother seems to have left and Harriet can't take care of her anymore, she's with us now," she said with an abruptness in her voice Frank had heard before when Mollie wanted something.

"That's all very fine but . . .," Frank said, knowing the child's mother would want her back when she returned.

"Now, Frank, don't be an old poop!" his wife said. She'd always called him an old poop when he didn't do as she thought should be done. They'd had a very happy life together, still in love and better, still in like, best friends after twenty-seven years of marriage. "But what?" she asked, looking him straight in the eye.

"You know what," he said, quietly adding, "And this little girl's mother will be wanting her back."

She looked down sadly and then looked up smiling, saying, "That was then, this is now." A quick remembrance flashed through her mind of another child that had so shortly graced their lives. It was three years ago, little James, whose mother had changed her mind just an hour before the judge was to make his decree saying James would become the son of Frank and Mollie. Mollie's body suddenly shook at the thought, giving her a chill. She'd fallen immediately in love with that little boy he looked so much like

Frank. She gave a quick prayer, begging God not to let it happen again, to somehow let little Betty stay with them. She didn't care how it would happen; she just wanted that little girl. She wouldn't be able to go through losing another child—it was just too hard—but now maybe a chance had come to bring Betty Gray permanently into their lives

"There has got to be some reason this is beginning to happen again. God wouldn't put three such strikes on us," she said.

"Mollie, you don't know anything about the circumstances of the child's situation," he said, looking over at Betty Gray. God, she was cute. He was hooked.

"I know, but Harriet and I are getting a room ready for her now," she said, not wanting to think of it.

"Mrs. Carey, I need help," Harriet called from upstairs.

"I'll go," Frank said, getting up. As he walked up the wide staircase carpeted by an oriental runner of an off-paisley design, he looked back into the living room at the baby girl still sitting on the couch watching him leave. He couldn't deny she was adorable, but he knew she had a family somewhere.

"Mr. Carey, would you be helping me assemble the crib? I'm not sure how we did it earlier," Harriet said, seeing him.

"Harriet, this is not a good idea. Mrs. Carey is going to get hurt all over again," he said sternly.

"I hope not. The wee one does need a roof over her head, and she's here now. I'd be just havin' a feeling, you know, that Irish leprechaun feeling I get sometimes when somethin' good is about to happen."

"I've heard you speak of it, but this is a serious matter. I don't want Mrs. Carey to get ideas that can't be, or to suffer over this. She's been through too much already," he said, looking at Harriet. Frank had a look, a strong, serious look about him. At times he was light and fun loving and gentle, but he was also deep, businesslike, and determined. He loved his wife—she was the mainstream of his life—and he'd do everything in his power to keep her calm and happy. He wasn't all business, and his gentler side couldn't go through the loss of another child. He was also sensitive, especially about this, but he liked this little girl propped up on the couch whom he'd spent time with a bit earlier.

"I also don't want her to suffer. She's not good at it, but I know the truth," Harriet said, putting the parts of the bed in the correct order on the floor. Picking up the headboard, she continued, "Would you be minding to be pickin' up the footboard. I'll be proppin' this one against the wall then we can get the sides attached," she kind of ordered. Naturally he followed her instructions. In fifteen minutes they had it all assembled and in the room. "We now need the mattress. Would yea be helping me bring it down?"

"Of course," he said, following her back up into the attic. It wasn't a heavy thing, just cumbersome for them to get around the corners. Finally they had it in place. Mollie came in with the bedding. Harriet quickly put the sheet on; it was ready. Betty was brought in to see her new room. They stood watching, wondering if the child liked their efforts.

"I'm very impressed with the two of you and your crib-assembly talent," Mollie said, looking at them.

"A piece of cake, nothing to it," Frank said. It's about three. Does she have to take a nap or something?"

"It's probably a good idea," Mollie agreed. She picked up the little girl and started to undress her, taking off her little dress and then shoes and socks and laying her in the crib on her back. She just cooed and gurgled a little, looking up at the ceiling with its flowers painted in a crisscross garland running from corner to corner. There was a small, delicate frosted-glass globe light hanging down from where the painted pink, cream, and red roses crossed. The walls were a soft cream. The floor was covered by a good light-green carpet. The furniture had belonged to Mrs. Carey's grandmother, Elizabeth Forbes Whittich, who had come from Scotland to the new country in 1840, only to die in childbirth after a short marriage to Frederich Whittich. She left behind Mollie's father, James, a husband, and a family back in Dundee.

Two twin sleigh beds made of a dark, almost black, oak; a dresser with a wide, tilting oval mirror; a tall chest of drawers with two small drawers on top and four larger, deeper drawers underneath; and a matching dark oak desk made up the furniture in the room. The late afternoon sun came through the lace tieback curtains of the window beside the desk; the other window was open, it's curtains slightly moving as though a fairy was pushing them, trying to get in to make its first official magic visit and introduction to the child.

"Frank, don't you think it would be a good idea to close that window? I don't want Betty catching a cold."

"Good idea." He walked over to the window, gently shutting it and glancing at Betty lying there. "Should we leave the door open?"

"Yes. We need to hear what she is doing or if she needs us," Mollie answered. "You know, I think we need a chair in here too, so I can rock and feed her."

"I'll get the small one from the library," Frank said, going out on his way to find and bring it. Mollie and Harriet quietly left behind him.

Five minutes later the chair was put beside the crib. Before he left, Frank leaned over and kissed Betty on top of her head. "I wish you could stay. You've already brought so much happiness," he whispered. A moment later he was downstairs.

"Now is there a kiss for this weary husband of yours?" he asked, taking Mollie in his arms. He loved the way she felt, soft like a woman, making him feel like a man.

"Always, a thousand," she answered, putting her mouth on his. As always it was a sweet and delicate kiss and then another.

"Darling, would you like to go out for dinner tonight to that little French café on Hennepin Avenue?" He could smell her perfume; she was everything he wanted, and he was so glad she'd married him.

"How can we? What about Betty" she said, feeling his heart beat as he held her. She always felt safe in Frank's arms; he was just the best man in the world, giving her everything she could ever have wanted and making their life so beautiful. She was still in love with him after twenty-seven years together.

"Harriet can stay with her. She knows about children and Betty knows her best. I really would like to take you out, and Betty is sleeping. Why don't you get your hat? We'll be back very soon," he whispered into her ear. "Well, all right, but only for a quick bite. I'll go ask Harriet to stay on a bit later today," she said, releasing him.

Harriet was found in the kitchen wiping out the inside of one of the drawers; she was quietly humming an Irish lullaby. Its pretty melody was endearing, making Mollie want Betty even more.

"That is such a pretty tune. Harriet, I'd like to ask a favor of you. Would you mind staying on a little longer today? Frank wants to take me to dinner. We'll be back soon. Could you possibly stay?" Mollie asked.

"Of course," Harriet agreed, smiling. She had nothing else to do; this would break up one of the long, lonely evenings of her life. She never thought she'd end up alone and so early, but that was the hand she was dealt.

"Thank you. We won't be gone long," Mollie assured her. She then went into the bedroom, opening her closet. She looked through the dresses hanging there. She chose the purple one, feeling like a queen at the moment. Twenty minutes later she'd put the last comb in her hair and finished applying a little face powder and just the lightest touch of rouge on her lips. She then put on the new hat Frank had given her for her birthday this year; it had the most gorgeous pink ostrich plumes and a lovely matching bow of dark pink velvet. She was a pretty, intelligent-looking woman with a heart of gold, five feet three inches tall, one hundred one pounds and stately in her demeanor. She loved reading, needlework, knitting, and children; but Frank Leighton Carey was the main point of her life. She wanted him to succeed. He was wonderful, and he deserved the best, and from her end of things, she'd make sure he got it. They were a good team.

While Mollie changed, Frank also freshened up. He liked style and gentle, gracious living, having a sense of class and sophistication given to him early in his life by his mother, the last lady in his family to leave Ireland, just a year before his birth.

"I'm ready," Mollie called to her husband.

"Let's go. My, you look beautiful."

Thank you. So do you."

Harriet waved to them as they drove out the driveway and down the street, wishing them a happy evening and telling them not to worry—she had everything under control.

The Chateau de Paris's entrance was very European-looking, with a thick wooden door and a large strong metal doorknob; three wide stone steps brought them into the restaurant. Once inside, a strong French atmosphere ruled; the feeling one got while a smell of good solid French cooking greeted them, awakening everyone's appetite. Light-yellow walls filled with a number of French posters advertising food, wines, and cities graced the large main dining room. Small tables covered by long white tablecloths and large matching napkins stood in slanted rows, holding clear glass goblets and shiny silverware. Each place setting had pretty white dinner plates bordered with small sweetly painted flowers in pink, blue, orange, and apricot; little green leaves danced between the flowers. They sat down to menus that were equally charming, with serious temptations inside. Before looking things over, Frank ordered kir for them; he thought the colors of the Cassis and white wine would cheer his wife. He was right. "Are you hungry?" he asked as he looked over his menu. Everything looked so good. Even though he wasn't terribly hungry he could taste each item listed. "Look, honey. They have filet of beef au poivre, rack of lamb persillade, Rouge de Flaugergues, and coquelles Saint Jacques. I just don't know what I want. What do you like?"

"It's kind of hard to make up my mind. The coquelles gratinées St. Michel, scallops with cheese and cream, looks very tempting—yes, that's what I want."

"Darling," Frank quietly said, raising his glass, " je t'aime."

"Je t'aime," she answered, smiling at all his kindness. Their glasses touched, making a sweet tinkling. The kir tasted so good she asked for another.

"Really? You're sure?" he said, planning on ordering another for himself in any case. "Let's live."

"Yes. You know I'm feeling better. Just being here in this lovely place with you, I feel revived."

"I'm glad. That was the idea. Do you suppose two glasses of kir have anything to do with it?" he asked, smiling at her. She was so pretty. He loved the subtle way she seemed to be changing—gentle streaks of a slight grayish white could be seen in between the soft brown color of her hair, and a demure smile line was beginning to form, marking her fun-loving spirit. Her skin had a lovely soft look, making her look younger than her years, and in this lighting he could see her eyes were getting a gentleness he hadn't noticed before.

"Probably. Kir is going to be my new tonic." She smiled back. "Really?" he joked.

"I think it is a great idea."

"You do?" he teased.

"Yes, why not?" she teased back

"I'll get the ingredients, and I'll make them for you at home."

"Would you?" She smiled

"Anything and everything for you," he said, taking her hand and bringing it up to his lips and kissing it. She smiled; he was just the best.

The waiter came then, asking if they were ready to order.

"I think so," Frank said. "My wife would like the coquilles gratinées, and I'd like the filet de boeuf en croute."

"Very good," the young waiter said, leaving them to finish their drinks.

"Frank, could Betty be ours?" Mollie asked all of a sudden. "I can't stop thinking about her."

"I don't think so. Her mother is not dead, and if she was it wouldn't be easy. It would most likely be a long and involved process involving lots of lawyers and probably lots of unpleasantness. Who knows what the story is there," he said, opening his napkin and putting it on his lap.

"I'm afraid of that. Let's do what we need to," she said, lifting her glass to take another sip. The kir was lovely.

"Okay, but don't hold your breath," he said, sipping his kir.

"To Betty, little Betty."

"I can drink to that," he said, looking over at Mollie and smiling. A serious note came to his voice. "I want you to be extremely strong and brave through what is about to begin. We may not get her. Her family is young, and most likely there are grandparents too. If we do get her, it would be wonderful, but if we don't, we still have each other, and that is the way it is supposed to be."

"I know. I'm going to pray we get her."

"We'll need all the help we can get. I'll go to see Stuart McCloud. He can suggest where to start." He took another sip.

"Good." She paused. "How can she be alone? Where is her family? Why doesn't anyone hear from them?"

"They probably don't know about her mother or they don't care. We also don't know about her mother. Is the family here in the Twin Cities or are they elsewhere? There are lots to be known before we can do anything. I'll talk to Stuart."

"Why does everything have to be so hard?" she sighed.

"I don't know, darling. It always seems to be, doesn't it?" he said, reaching over to hold her hand. They sat silently holding each other's hand until the food came, brightening the mood.

"This looks so good. I'm starved," Frank said as the aroma of properly cooked beef came into his nostrils. He smiled down at the plate. Taking his knife and fork, he made a strong solid cut into the meat, bringing a good piece into his mouth. "Hmm."

"Mine too. The scallops look absolutely perfect," she said, putting one into her mouth. After swallowing, she had one word for her dinner—heavenly.

Forty-five minutes later, they paid the bill. Frank had decided to take Mollie for a leisurely ride. He wanted to talk about life with the baby; he wanted to know what she wanted him to do. He wanted to tell her how happy he was about Betty coming into their lives.

"Having Betty with us is going to be so nice," he started.

"Yes. She's such a sweet child. I already love her more than I could know," Mollie said.

"Me too. I think Harriet should have a nice raise. She'll be nanny now too."

"I agree. Would five hundred dollars a year more be all right?"

"That sounds very fair. I'll tell her about it soon."

"Oh, Frank, you're so wonderful. How could this luck have come to us? Poor Mrs. Leveroos to leave her child," Mollie said, thinking that Harriet had brought a miracle, that all the grief from lost sons was in the past, and this precious little girl was everything she could want. God's grace felt so good. She hoped there wouldn't be any problems since Betty's family couldn't be found. She prayed there would be no surprises.

I want to go shopping tomorrow. We need so many things now—clothes, bottles, toys . . . how about a pet? A cat or dog?" she asked, looking over at her husband and new father.

"I'd love for Betty to have a pet, but let's wait a while. I want her to adjust to us, then we can think about a dog," Frank said, smiling at how fun all of this seemed and how happy his wife was.

"Of course you're right. She needs to adjust to us and her new surroundings. I wonder how much babies realize about what is going on around them? Will she notice her mother isn't taking care of her?" Mollie asked with a little jealousy forming.

"I'm sure she will, but as the days go by, she'll forget about Helen. Sad, isn't it, a child can forget its natural mother."

"Yes, but I'll make up for that. She's going to have a new mother and father who are crazy about her, a new home, and new friends."

"I don't know who is luckier, her or us," Frank said, looking at the vast city before him. It was growing by leaps and bounds. He realized one day the whole country would be a huge place filled with such golden opportunities that have never been seen before in history. The country would be changing when the war was finished, and he wanted to be part of it. Technology was improving everything, and all the time and the grain business was going to benefit by this in every way.

"Life with a baby is going to be very different. No more doing just what we please, going out whenever we want to. No more quiet evenings just the two of us. Now there will be toys and noise and clutter around all the time. Are you ready?"

"Bring on the noise and clutter. We've been living in a tomb too long." He laughed at the thought; she did too.

They got home around nine, and Frank was tired, but he wanted to take Harriet home before he settled in for the night. He was glad to finally put the car in the garage, open the door, and sit down to read the newspaper.

While Frank took Harriet home, Mollie had gone up to check on Betty and to get undressed. She found Betty sleeping so sweetly that when he got back she called him up to see her.

"Look at our precious one. God, I love her. Have you ever seen anyone sleep like that?" Mollie whispered.

"How could anyone be so dear?" he asked, taking Mollie's hand, adding, "Boy, am I bushed. I hope I'll sleep like that tonight."

"You probably will."

They walked out of Betty's room and into their own and got into bed. Frank fell asleep right away; Mollie lay awake listening for sounds of her baby. She wanted to be ready in case Betty needed something, then she too fell asleep.

Chapter 3

Earlier, as Frank took his black Pierce Arrow with its elegant gray cloth seats out of the garage to take Harriet home, Helen slowly packed her suitcase. There was a twinge of regret about the opportunity to leave the show, but mostly she was glad; she'd prepared her whole life for this chance, and now Hollywood was at hand. Eileen Elliot, her understudy, needed a break. Even though Eileen didn't have Helen's sense of the part, Helen thought she was good, but that's where it ended. *Hamlet* was a beautiful work and had given Helen a chance to portray drama in its classic form. Ophelia was a demanding role, but not too much. It let her use her skill to show madness, depression, and feelings from the gut, bringing Ophelia to full life; but a new opportunity had come: the movies called.

She felt a strong twinge of guilt that she hadn't told Harriet of the glorious chance, but in the slight case she didn't make it, she didn't want anyone rubbing her nose in the failure, so off she went. She loved Betty Gray, but Harriet was there and Betty knew her. She figured if it should turn out Harriet couldn't keep Betty Gray, possibly the family she worked for could. Her plan was in motion.

Socially prominent and financially well-off, Helen knew the Careys were a good choice for her daughter. Of the little she knew of them, she was most struck not by their money but that they'd lost five sons, all babies. Possibly they'd like a little girl. She cringed at the thought of this pain. Who more likely would want a child? It almost seemed like some sort of theater piece. The night before she left, she'd told Betty of her plan.

"Is Mama's little sweetheart ready for bed?" Helen looked at her little girl sitting in the middle of a blanket on the floor. She still couldn't get over how cute her daughter was and how much she looked like Goff. It was easy to see who Betty's father was—the same nose, the same hairline, the same expression, definitively a chip off the old block. Helen couldn't see much of herself in Betty; maybe when her personality and intellect emerged she'd see herself.

Picking up the little girl, she carried her over to her little bed, gently laying her on her back. Betty smiled up at her mother, waving her hands at her. "Sweetheart, Mama has got a big chance to be in the movies. You know we've been waiting for something like this . . . well, it's finally come," she gently said, smiling. "Mama's agent, Brian, told me about a chance to go to Hollywood, but I'll have to give up the role of Ophelia. I'm sorry about this. He says there is a role for me in a big film. So that is what Mama is going to do. Auntie Harriet, the lady across the hall you like so much will take care of you. It's all okay. Can you imagine me in a film in Hollywood? Betty, your mama is going to be in lots of films and a big famous star. Don't worry, Mama will do her best, and then in a little while, Daddy will be coming home, and we'll be together again. I wonder what he'll think of me as a film star. He'll be so happy. In the meantime, I want you to stay with Auntie Harriet, to be a good girl, and don't worry about anything." She began to sing a little lullaby.

Betty Gray listened to the sound of her mother's voice as she spoke, not realizing her life was about to take a major turn. Slowly she drifted off, leaving her Helen to muse alone about her new career as a big film star. She knew her career would take off; she knew she had what was required and the fortitude to get and keep herself there. She also knew the days in St. Paul would be in her past. She was going forward and so was her child. She truly didn't feel she was abandoning Betty. Her conscience was clear about it, and she'd told Betty Gray she'd be back—then they'd make up for the time lost. This career move was based on not only her desire and talent but Goff being away so long in the war, the Leverooses' attitude, and the insult she felt when they denied her financial help when she asked. Helen had always felt excluded by Goff's family. She knew she wasn't their type of folk, even though her family did own the Taylor Drugstore and had done very well.

Helen was artistic, having feelings and sensitivity they didn't. They were snooty, believing theater people were part of the lower society (they weren't), but the Leverooses, with their haughty attitude about certain things, stood firm.

It was the last straw when, a little later, her own father also denied her the money she needed for Betty Gray because they didn't like Goff. This brought her to realize Betty Gray would be better off eventually with the

Careys, and she'd come to them through Harriet. She remembered Harriet had mentioned she worked for them and of the intense unhappiness they had at being childless because of the death of all their sons. Yet Frank and Mollie were older. *Would that matter?* she wondered. A quick thought told her no, it didn't matter at all.

A thought about her agent Brian came. He wasn't a nice man, twenty years her senior; he was a me kind of person. Balding and plump, he shoved and welded his way around the theater world. By age forty he had three wives, each one kicking herself for falling for his convincing, energetic, haughty, and, in the beginning, concealed arrogant attitude, which only slowly revealed itself a little too late for them.

With all his flaws, everyone wanted him as their agent. He had a marvelous ability to create strong relationships with actresses because they knew he was the best at arranging lots of work, bringing fame and the money that went along with it, and bringing them quickly up the ladder of success. Now his ego was pumped up that Hollywood wanted his girl Helen, and the money they offered wasn't bad either, so the best of two worlds came to together: art and money.

"Helen, I've got wonderful news," he said two nights ago.

"Really? What's up?" she asked.

"Remember I told you three weeks into the *Hamlet* run that movie scout Jimmy Pool had been in town?"

"Yes, vaguely," she said, looking at his square jaw and massive strong teeth.

"He saw the show and, after, told me he liked your look and command of the stage."

"I'm honored."

"He talked about a new film he was casting, which will begin shooting in about a month. He wants you, Helen. He wants you," Brian said, his big teeth sparkling as was his pride.

"What does he want me for?"

"For the second lead. The part of Pamela."

"That's wonderful, but I couldn't just up and leave this show," she said with a little concern in her voice.

"I think it would be okay," he said in a tone signifying he had inside knowledge.

"How's that? Every night I get a standing ovation. I bring them in."

"As I'm sure you've heard or noticed, director Jack's having a serious affair with Eileen."

"Yes, I noticed. Everyone noticed. I'm not surprised. He's had several since we started this production. It goes along with the territory, and his nature, I guess."

"Probably. Lord knows what serious means here, but I guess she's been after him about giving her the Ophelia part, and he's looking for a way to let you go."

"Really! Just like that? Jack is a talented director, but I see he's an equally talented jerk. Eileen for me? Ridiculous! And he's already talked to you? Eileen for me? Boy is he making a mistake!" She kind of laughed, almost giggled, at the idea.

"Yeah. So if you want to come on board for this film . . ."

"Eileen to replace me! Me! This show would be no place without me, you'll see. I'm the best," she said, her ego showing itself for the first time to Brian. She tossed her head, not in a vulgar way but in one of confidence. "You'll have to go to Los Angeles. The auditions are on the seventeenth.

I know you're great, and I'm so sure you'll get it." He smiled, ignoring the toss of her head, which he took to be an arrogant stand, something artistic people sometimes have. It made him feel important to be the discoverer of a potential big film star.

"Love is a funny thing. So Eileen is having a roll in the hay with our director Jack. I can act circles around her. Good. I wonder what the pay is," she said, looking straight at him.

"Then you really want to do it?" he asked, looking at her. He liked looking at her face; she was pretty and warm looking. He could see confidence and determination.

"It's beginning to sound very interesting. Yes, I want it! Of course I want it. I've waited my whole life for this. When?" She smiled broadly now as her head danced with the thought of the opportunity. At that second, she was glad little Eileen and Jack were together. They deserved each other, not that it mattered.

She was more than happy to go soon, to Los Angeles, for an audition. She understood they needed to know how she photographed and looked on the screen before the shoot began.

"Oh, on the seventeenth, okay," he said.

As Helen's thoughts sang, a different thought crept into her brain—what to do about Betty? Harriet—yes, her neighbor. Harriet, with her connections, was the answer. Problem solved. With Harriet's help she could be free to become the star she thought she could be. She was good. Everyone from the third grade to now said so.

Chapter 4

Frank was feeling good as he got to his office. The grain business is what he knew and loved. It had been a good and nicely prosperous business, giving him enough money to enjoy their beautiful home on wonderful Lake of the Isles. Mollie's friend Alice Green had lived in the house before them. Several years ago she decided to move to her son and his family in California. When Frank heard her house was up for sale, he bought it for Mollie. He'd been a little worried it would be too big for them, but he knew Mollie would love to live in her best friend's home. Now since they were to have a child, this wonderfully big house with its big yard had been the right choice—no regrets.

"I'm sorry to be so late . . . had some family business to take care of. Are the last quarter figures from Montana here? I need to check those and the grain impact figures for today, and those from Iowa. Would you bring them into my office?" he asked, looking at his oftentimes very overworked secretary, Rose.

"I'll get them for you right away, Mr. Carey."

At that he went to his desk to start the work of the day, but as he worked, thoughts of the little girl he wanted to be his daughter were on the back of his mind.

At six that evening, he opened the door and was welcomed home with hugs and kisses from Mollie.

"How was your day?" she whispered.

"Full and busy," he said, taking off his coat. "Can I make you a drink? Where's Betty?"

"I'd love one. She's in her room sleeping. I'm surprised how much babies sleep," she said, taking his coat and hanging it in the front closet.

"We have a lot to learn. How about bourbon and soda? That's what I'm having," he quietly said, going to the dining room where they had a semibar on the buffet.

"Okay, please," she kind of whispered. "Bourbon with soda water was always a good drink."

"Coming right up," he said, taking two glasses from the left-side cabinet of the brown buffet. Carefully he poured in two fingers worth of bourbon in his glass but only one for Mollie, thinking it interesting that since her last pregnancy she'd completely changed from drinking white wine to bourbon. Next he filled them nearly to the top with bubbling club soda.

Taking the drinks into the living room and handing her one, he toasted, "To the future."

"To the future," she repeated, taking a sip.

The rest of the evening was spent in the ordinary things of domestic life: dinner and Frank playing on the melodeon "Frankie and Johnnie" and "After the Ball," and tonight he added, "Come of Your Buttercup Buy" from Gilbert and Sullivan's *H.M.S. Pinafore*. Mollie fed Betty once more, and he read the newspaper to her, and then they went to bed, but not before checking once again on Betty. Tomorrow Mollie wanted to listen to the new records of Brahms's *Academic Overture* that Frank bought last week; music had a way of making the weight of the world leave her for a while. She often thanked God for his gift of the invention of music.

Once in bed, Frank held her close, caressing her shoulder and arms. "I went to see Stuart McCloud today."

"Oh. How is he? What did he have to say?" she said, turning toward him. She could feel his warmth against her; it was so nice.

"He mainly said he wasn't able to help but said we could talk to the Leverooses if we could find them and felt it would help. He didn't think it would serve much purpose. He also sends you his regards."

"That's very nice of him. I kind of thought that might be the case. I still want to know something about them."

"Me too," he whispered, kissing her shoulder.

"You know the easiest way to get to know about them is through Harriet," he said.

"I'll ask her about it tomorrow," Mollie said, starting to yawn. "Sweet dreams, darling."

"And to you too. I love you, Mrs. Carey," he said, gripping her shoulder a little tighter.

"I love you too. I think it's all going to be good," she said turning on her back.

The night went by quickly, eased away by a beautiful sunny morning. Mollie couldn't wait to see Betty, to hold, kiss, and be her mother. She also could hardly wait to talk to Harriet. Quickly she dressed the baby and herself and then went downstairs to make coffee and hot cereal for them, putting Betty between several pillows on the floor, keeping her near. Harriet arrived just as they'd finished eating. Frank also had finding baby family information on his mind for the day, but before that could start, he had to go to the office to see if more figures from Montana had come. He greeted Harriet as she came in, kissing Mollie and Betty as he went out. "Mornin', Mrs. Carey. 'Tis a lovely day to be singin' the Lord's praises,"

Harriet said, smiling brightly at them. "Yes, indeed."

"I see you've had your breakfast. Could I be makin' you another coffee?"

"Please, that would be very nice. As you can guess I've still got the Leveroos family on my mind."

"Me too," she said, pouring fresh water into the coffee pot and getting a handful of coffee beans ready to be put into the grinder on the wall. She knew she probably didn't need to grind any more beans, but she wanted the coffee as fresh as she could make it, the same she felt about her baking. She was proud of her kitchen skills and liked to share in her labor. "The poor dears."

"Yes, how sad, especially for the baby."

"Poor darlin'. Just imagine leavin' a sweet baby girl," Harriet said.

"It's dreadful. Do you have anything else to tell me about them?"

"Well, I've heard from Mrs. Dodd that the father was a handful when he was young, a teenager, you know," Harriet said.

"What happened?"

"Things were strained between him and his parents. Apparently, when he was in his teens, he ran off with some girl and married her. He was seventeen and she was only fifteen."

"Really!" Mollie was shocked. She'd never heard of anything like that before.

"Yes. When Mr. Leveroos Sr.—his name is Bert—found out, he ran after them, brought them back, and got the marriage annulled right then."

"My goodness. What happened to the girl?" Mollie asked, still stunned at what she'd heard.

"She went back to her family, but it was so hard keepin' them apart even though the girl's family threatened to charge Goff with rape. Then his father got his lawyer involved. After some negotiations were made and some money paid, the girl's family packed up and moved to Ohio. Bert enrolled Goff in a military boarding school in Georgia."

"The Leverooses are quite well-off due to their fine men's clothing store in St. Paul. All they needed was for someone in the family to be charged with rape. That kind of thing would have ruined them and maybe ended their business. The old man, Bert, wouldn't allow such a thing to destroy what he built. He was as proud as a man could be. His son was as equally free-spirited," Harriet said, looking at Mollie's reaction.

"Very interesting. So who is Betty's mother?" Mollie asked. A little tremble in her voice told Harriet she really wanted to know, but didn't.

"Sometime after boarding school, Goff met Helen Taylor, probably at the theater. She was an actress from Stillwater, Minnesota. They were married in 1915, and Betty was born the next February."

"An actress, ugh. Who are her people?" Mollie asked as she put Betty on her lap.

"I haven't heard anything about them," Harriet said, looking at them. They looked so sweet together. "They don't seem to be around here, even though there are lots of Taylors."

"I'd really like to know as much about them as possible."

"I'll keep my ears open. I can ask Mrs. Dodd. Maybe she can tell me more," Harriet said.

That night, after a light supper, Harriet casually walked to the Dodd house.

Sally Dodd saw Harriet in the window. They waved as she turned into the walkway.

"Mrs. Oates, how nice to see you," Mrs. Dodd said as she opened the door. "Please come in. It's been some time since you were here last."

"Ah, that's true. Thank you. I'm sorry to be coming unannounced. I've been awfully busy with Mrs. Carey. Poor dear's been havin' a tough time of late."

"It's quite all right. I'm sorry to hear that. What about you? How are you?" Sally Dodd looked at Harriet, thinking she looked the same. She went into the kitchen to put the kettle on. As Harriet followed, she, as always, looked around the living room and at the dining room as they passed through both to get to the kitchen. The living room had an air about it that she felt had too much spit and polish, making her feel they never used the room. It was beautifully decorated with yellow, light green, and purple flowered moiré curtains, which elegantly framed each of the three large windows that looked out onto the street. In front of the windows was a large tufted tan leather couch; two matching Queen Anne chairs sat at an angle at each end of the couch. Mrs. Dodd had a lovely white marble-topped table sitting in front of the couch. A large desk on the opposite wall was filled with several opened letters, a bottle of ink, two pens, a blotter, and a small stamp box. A very pretty petite desk chair with a tufted yellow moiré seat sat in front of the desk. It looked like a wonderful place for writing. There were two medium-sized oriental rugs filling the floor space and an ordinary fireplace screen with brass and irons and matching tools sitting at the end of the room off to the left. To the right of the fireplace was a full wood box, also in brass. The white walls held several flower paintings, and above the fire place was a lovely portrait of an old-fashioned-looking lady, probably Sally Dodd's grandmother—it fit the room.

The dining room had a large baroque-patterned wall paper in dark green and gold. The furniture was heavy looking; a dark wooden table with four chairs covered in forest-green velvet sat around the table. A matching buffet stood against the wall near the kitchen, which was draped with a white doily edged in gathered lace, giving it a wavy look. A number of silver serving pieces sat on the buffet, and two large candlesticks were placed on the table near the center. A stack of freshly ironed napkins and a nicely folded white tablecloth sat on the table, waiting for Mrs. Dodd to put them away.

"I'm just fine but am worried about Mrs. Carey," Harriet said.

"I have two teas today, Earl Grey and Lipton. Which would you prefer?" Sally Dodd asked, changing the subject. Looking at her neighbor, she also thought Harriet looked the same.

"Earl Grey, please. The Careys are thinking of adopting a little girl, the Leverooses' girl, Betty Gray," Harriet said.

"Oh!" Sally paused. "I'm also in the mood for Earl Grey today," she said, getting the metal tea box out of the cupboard, opening it, taking out the required amount of tea, and putting it in a small bowl. She then put water into her large copper tea kettle and put it on the stove to boil. She added, "Why would they be interested in her?"

"You haven't heard? Mrs. Leveroos has up and left, not a word said. The child needs a new home," Harriet told her as she started things. Harriet loved Sally's tea service. The beautiful flowers so nicely painted on each cup put her in a better mood, not to mention the tea itself smelled so wonderful—just what she needed. She was beginning to like Mrs. Dodd. A thought of inviting her to her home one day passed through her mind. "Really! I hadn't heard. I wonder why. She was a nice lady. I never paid any mind to her being an actress. I know others did, but I didn't. In fact I liked her," Mrs. Dodd said.

"She was an actress?" Harriet was shocked.

"Yes. She was performing in *Hamlet* at the Strand Theater. My friend Daisy and I went to the performance last night and were very disappointed when an understudy came on instead," Mrs. Dodd said.

"My, my. She's an actress. That's very interesting," Harriet said as if to put the idea into perspective.

"Yes, and a very good one. I've seen her on several occasions, and she was always able to make me feel something. She's quite a good comic too. Her mother, Gloria Taylor, was also an actress in the local theater world and was a big name. She died about a year ago of a massive heart attack right onstage. It really scared the audience, not to mention the other actors and crew. I've seen Helen twice, and I think she was even better than her mother. She should really be in the movies. They're the big thing now," Mrs. Dodd explained.

"That's interesting. She's an actress?" she questioned again, this time with a bit of hesitation, surprised that this lady had any interest in an actress or the local theater.

"Mrs. Leveroos is pretty, with lovely gray-blue eyes and rich, thick light-brown hair. Sometimes she seemed somewhat away from things, in another world. I understand artists can be like that," Harriet said.

"What about the child?"

"She's with me for the moment," Harriet said, not mentioning the Careys. "That's good," Mrs. Dodd said. "Mrs. Leveroos often asked me to take care of the child for the evening while she performed. It wasn't too often. She didn't work much, two or three plays a year. She was always home no later than eleven. During the performance time she often seemed distracted—actually she seemed off in another world. I think she was proud to have followed in her mother's steps. I saw her mother perform twice, and I think Helen was better," Sally said.

"My goodness. She was an actress," Harriet said, again having a hard time visualizing her neighbor in that capacity.

"Mrs. Leveroos was pretty, gentle, but seemed somewhat sad at times. I always thought she was too well-dressed for her circumstances." Her tone seemed to change as she spoke. "Made me wonder how she could afford the clothes she had," Mrs. Dodd said, her female duty to gossip uncontrollably leaping out.

"How did she seem toward the little girl?" Harriet asked, wondering if she had been at all like actresses one hears of, notorious like Isadora Duncan or Sarah Bernhardt.

"I must say she seemed very loving. When she put her in my arms and started to walk out the door she'd come running back hugging and kissing the child saying again, 'I'll be back soon. You be a good girl.' Then she'd go out the door waving," she said, her mood and attitude mellowing.

"Did she ever talk about her husband?" she asked as she looked over to see if the water was boiling.

"Oh yes, often. She loved him very much. She hated that the navy sent him off to the war. She worried he would be wounded over there. And she never spoke of her in-laws. Her husband has two sisters, Emily and Ebba, but I never heard anything about them. They were older. I don't know anything about her family. I guess her husband being away, trying to take care of their child, her mother's death, and making money as a secretary to support them must have put a lot of pressure on her. It's always about money, isn't it? I guess working in the theater gave her relief."

"I wonder why she'd leave."

"Maybe it was a combination of everything."

At least the one good factor brought out a strong sense of Harriet wanting Mollie and Frank Carey to take over Betty's life. This passion shot through her being like an unexpected wind coming out of nowhere, surprising her. They needed that little girl, but she needed them even more. Somehow this desire for the Careys to have the baby put whatever the Leveroos family's desires might have been right out of her mind.

"Yes," Mrs. Dodd said in agreement, adding the tea to the nicely boiling water. She stirred it a bit then let it steep for another few moments.

Chapter 5

    Helen Taylor, Mrs. Godfrey Leveroos in her private life, gingerly climbed the few steps up onto the train headed for California. It pulled out of the depot at five forty-two, as its normal schedule directed. It was a lovely evening for travel—it wasn't raining, it wasn't snowing, just a nice evening to take a train trip. The porter showed her to her compartment. There wasn't much room, but Helen didn't mind. She was on her way to something big. She put her suitcase up on the shiny metal luggage rack, took off her coat, and put it on the hook beside the rack. Sitting down, she noticed the lovely softness of the velvet-covered seat and how clean and clear the window was.

    Slowly the train started with a little jerk; several big puffs of smoke came from the smoke stack, which billowed into the sky. Slowly it made its way west. Leaving Minneapolis, it went through the northern part of America, later making its way southwest to California. By the next morning they were speeding along at a good clip. She liked listening to the rhythmic clicking of the wheels on the tracks and watching the scenery slowly change. She'd bought Bozidar Arandjelovic's first translated book, *Thundering Blue Skies*, at the depot and quickly became consumed by his way with words, which pulled her into his story and mind. California was soon at hand, but not before Arandjelovic put her in another world.

    Helen had said good-bye to Betty and put her in Harriet's capable hands. As she read Arandjelovic, thoughts about the little lullaby she'd sang to Betty the night before came into her mind. It was a sweet little song her mother had sung to her. The rocking and rolling of the train was an unfamiliar feeling, but it was part of getting to her new life. She began to think about all she'd given up—well, not exactly given up but put aside, on hold. The opportunity to be in a film and the second lead was just too good to pass up. The theater, acting, being up on that stage, whispered to her as thoughts of fame and fortune mulled in her mind. Remembrance of the most beautiful words an actress could want to hear—"Brava, brava, brava"—sang in her thoughts. *Hamlet* had been a wonderful experience.

"Helen, darling, you were marvelous tonight," the director of the show she'd done before *Hamlet*, *A Cold Night in July*, gushed as he excitedly burst into the shared dressing room. "No one could have played Mary like you. You're going to make us all rich and famous."

This play was everything Neil knew it would be. Jules Winston had written a masterpiece, and Helen had brought it to life. She had the talent, temperament, and look for the part. Hearing Neil's words brought a quick remembrance of the first time she'd heard the word *brava*. It had been shouted out by her mother and aunt when she was in the second grade doing her first role, as a snowflake. She smiled at the thought. The play that had brought her to Neil's attention was a high school production in her senior year, an imaginary discussion between Elizabeth I and Mary Queen of Scots called *E and M*. It had been a true challenge but a good learning tool.

Neil Storm had come to St. Paul to visit his sister for a few days five years ago, just to get away from the rat race of New York for a short time. They'd gone to the high school that night. Sitting in the dark theater he saw Helen's stage power as she portrayed Elizabeth I. Even through her extreme youth and inexperience, it was obvious she had that special something that puts one person ahead of another. She had what it took to be a star. He went backstage to talk to her.

"Miss Taylor. My name is Neil Storm. I'm an acting agent and director," he said, offering his hand.

"Hello. Did you like the show?" she asked, still on a rush from the performance.

"Very much. I liked your performance," he said, looking her straight in the eye.

"Thank you. I love being on stage. It makes me feel alive."

"I could see." He paused. "I represent several young people at the moment—Claire Ulman, Billie Dove, Steven Benz to name a few. There's a place for you, if you're interested. Oh, my card," he said, handing over a card with fancy business-looking writing.

"Oh my! What do I have to do?" She looked at the card, stroking it a little, almost as though it were a lucky rabbit's foot.

"Not much. Just let me represent you," he said.

That was two years ago, before Goff Leveroos. Now it was early 1917 and she was in St. Paul with a baby girl, longing for her former life.

Helen came from a good family. She'd done well in school, and at age nineteen had fallen seriously in love with the son of the owner of St. Paul's most elegant men's store, Godfrey Leveroos. Goff's parents had come to America from Sweden, ending up in St. Paul in 1880. They had three other children, three girls, Winifred, Emily and Ebba, and a good life primarily due to the successful way Bertram Leveroos had run things and taken care of his family. He was a no-nonsense-type person. Hard work and more of it, ethics, and a strong respect for the law and God formed the core of his life. In the new country he'd given his children freedom to pursue life in any way they chose. That was the reason they'd come to America. He'd put his son in boarding school to have him grow up. Later Goff had chosen a very pretty wife; now he was off on a ship, fighting the war, one of hundreds of sailors, just trying to obey orders and survive the terrible noise and fear from the conflicts they came upon.

Helen thought back on how she'd been busy with Betty and rehearsal for another play. She'd lost out on three juicy roles while she was pregnant, all of which she knew could have brought her to the attention of the local Minneapolis critics. That's all she needed—a little public recognition. Theater was in her blood, like a disease. No one else in her family had this inclination, but the acting bug had bitten her hard.

Thinking further back, she remembered the night she met Goff. She'd gone with her sister Anne and her boyfriend, Bill Webster, to the monthly dance at the St. Paul Hotel. It was an elegant place full of fine furniture upholstered in rich fabrics. Lovely paintings graced the walls of the lobby; many more were positioned throughout the building. The place had an air of making one feel important but just a little out of place. There wasn't a sense of don't touch," but almost, even though people felt at home.

Walking into the large ballroom, the band was playing "Sweet Alice Blue Gown." Such pretty music filled the beautiful white room trimmed in gold. A large chandelier and matching sconces gave subtle, almost romantic lighting to the evening. They were seated at a table off to the left, fairly close to the band. The room started to fill up. An older couple got the table on their right and another younger group on their right. Everyone was finely dressed. Suits, ties, and well-polished shoes for the men and beautifully styled dresses in every color of the rainbow for the women. Helen wore a gown of light blue and white organza. She had a beautiful snow-white silk gardenia pinned to the middle of her bodice, somewhat covering her décolletage. Her thick light-chestnut blonde hair was combed into the latest style as was Anne's. Anne had chosen a stripped beige and black silk skirt and matching beige silk blouse for the evening. By chance they both wore a rose-scented fragrance. Once seated, to the right, but down from the band, Bill ordered drinks for everyone—lemonade for the girls and beer for himself. Everyone politely clapped as the song ended. A moment later, they started to play another popular song.

Goff Leveroos sat, with several of his navy buddies on leave, across and to the left of Helen's table. They'd gotten there earlier to check out the young ladies as they arrived. When Helen came in, Goff's eye was drawn to the pretty girl with the light-chestnut hair. He intensely watched her as she walked with Anne and Bill to their table.

Who is she? he wondered.

"Hey, Goff, look there, the lady in beige. She's a beauty," his navy brother and school friend Walt Berman said with excitement.

"I see. Who's she with?"

"I don't know," Bob Joha said, also looking in Helen's direction, adding, "Wish I knew who she is."

"Me too. She seems so . . .," Walt piped in.

"Me too. I think I'm going to ask her to dance," Goff said, anxious for the next song to begin.

"Good idea," Bob agreed.

"Oh no. I'm going over there and ask her," Goff said.

Bob just looked at him. He knew he'd lose out. Goff was so good-looking and a good dancer. As chance would have it, the first notes of his favorite song started. He walked over to the other table and politely asked the young lady in blue to dance. As their eyes met, their hearts beat faster. He was handsome, she was beautiful, and they were drawn to each other at that second, without either of them realizing their futures were sealed. "I'd love to," she said, looking up at his blue eyes, warmly smiling. As she took his large hand, she could feel he was a strong man, with good character, she hoped.

He led them to the dance floor where "After the Ball's" beautiful melody had also brought other couples to the floor. He took her into his arms, bringing her very close to him.

"It's pretty music. This is my favorite song," he told her and then added, "What's your name?"

"Helen Taylor."

"Helen, that's a very pretty name," he said, looking at her petite hand as he gently whirled her to the one-two-three rhythm of the waltz.

"Thank you. What's your name?" she asked, looking up at the six-foot-tall, well-dressed young man. She liked the way he danced. He made her feel almost on air. This man had a sense of timing and polish. He knew how to make her feel as though they'd danced together a thousand times, instead of this being the first time.

"Goff Leveroos," he answered, liking the way she was able to follow his lead.

"Are you any relation to the Flon and Leveroos Men's Store?"

"One and the same. It's my father's store," he said, starting a turn.

"It's a pretty swanky store," she said, following the turn.

"You think so?"

"Yes. My father has bought several suits there."

"It's a nice store. We've had it for over twenty years. What do you do?" he asked as another young lady swished by him.

"I'm an actress. Actually I'm just beginning, but I've been in a lot of plays. I love being up there on the stage portraying different women. It's lots of fun," she answered, wondering what his reaction to the knowledge of her being on the stage would be. She hoped he wouldn't let the morals of the day—saying actresses were loose or something worse—affect him.

"That's interesting. I've never met an actress before," he said, leading her into another turn.

"Did you work in your father's store?"

"I did for a while, but it was boring. I need work that is more active, that gets me out. My father had me join the navy. He thinks I should help in the war effort, to get rid of those damn Huns. You know that's what they're being called now," Goff said, looking down at her hair, smelling the fragrance brought up from her perfume. The rose scent seemed to fit her.

"I'd heard that. Why don't they just call them what they are?"

"They're the enemy. They have to be called something bad," he said, surprised by her statement. Usually the girls didn't have anything to say about the war. It was all supposed to be over soon anyway.

"I hope you don't get hurt or killed," she said out of the blue. He liked the concern he thought he'd heard.

"Helen, that's so nice of you. I don't want to get hurt or killed either." She began to make him feel important.

"When did you join up?"

"Several months ago, but I don't want to think about it. Right now I want to concentrate on you," he said, still smelling the lovely rose perfume. "Are you in a show now?"

Helen blushed and smiled. No one had said anything like that to her before. She loved the compliment. She was happy with his attention and interest, but surprising to her, she felt somewhat shy. She wasn't shy about being on the stage, but strangely enough this moment made her feel insecure. He seemed to rule things, to be in charge, making her think of her father, but different, less demanding. It was nice. No other man she knew was like that.

"Not at the moment. Tomorrow I'm going for an audition."

"What show is it?"

"*Roses Are Red*. It was written by a couple from Minneapolis. They want it performed for the Women's Club," she said. "There are two good parts, sisters. I could do either one," she said, thinking about the audition. She really wanted the role of the older sister, Terry, but to play Paula would also be good.

"You seem so confident." He liked the way she talked, explaining things, making him want to know more about her and what she did.

"I think I am. I just need to show the director."

"I'm sure you'll do just fine," he said, glad to be the one dancing with her.

"I'll do my best. We'll see."

"I'll keep my fingers crossed."

She smiled. God, he was nice. Tomorrow's audition really would be okay. She could feel it in her bones.

"Will you come to see the show?"

"I'd like to. You'll have to tell me when and where to come."

Helen wanted the feeling of having a special place with him that was hers alone. Even though they were new, his arms were that place, and she knew she wanted to stay there.

A moment later, "After the Ball" ended; and quickly the music started again, this time a Straus waltz, one from *Die Fledermaus*. Its romantic feeling put them in a special mood, again letting them dance to the rhythm offered by the music. He kept her close. As the dance ended he found himself caught up in the passion of the moment. She was so pretty and soft. His desire began to burn. Before leaving the dance floor, he quickly but gently kissed her. It just seemed natural, but there was no denying the power of that kiss.

"Oh, I'm sorry," he stammered.

She didn't say anything.

"I don't want to offend you," he stammered again, afraid all would be lost. "I just couldn't help myself."

"You haven't offended me. On the contrary, I've just been given a second beautiful compliment." Looking into his eyes, she was glad of the kiss. Being kissed by a fine man is something every woman wants, but all of a sudden, like a bolt of lightning, she wondered if this sailor thought of her as cheap or loose. She was neither.

"I'd like to meet your friends. Let me take you back to your table," he said, totally unaware of her worry about him thinking she might somehow be low-class.

"I'm with my sister Anne and her boyfriend Bill," she said, taking his hand.

When they arrived Bill stood up. He was a tall, thin, distinguished-looking fellow with a small moustache, dressed in a plaid tan jacket and brown pants.

"Anne and Bill, I'd like you to meet Goff Leveroos."

"Pleased to meet you," Bill said, extending his hand.

Goff took it, giving a friendly handshake in return. He smiled over at Anne, nodding to her, and then said to Bill, "I'm happy to meet you."

"Thank you. Come and join us," Anne said, smiling at Goff. She thought he was awfully tall.

"All right, but just for a moment. My friends are waiting for me over there." He pointed.

After ten minutes of chitchat, Goff took Helen back to meet his friends.

"Helen Taylor, I'd like you to meet Walt Berman and Bob Joha. We're all in this thing together."

They both stood up as she extended her hand to each of them.

"Would you like a drink?" Bob offered.

"Thank you, but I couldn't. I should be getting back," Helen said, feeling a little anxious about leaving Anne and Bill. She'd always been somewhat timid, never having been left alone in life to do exactly as she pleased, except working in the theater.

"I'm sorry you can't stay. It was nice to meet you," Bob said as Walt chimed in with the same.

"Bye. Have a nice evening." Helen smiled at both of them.

Goff took her back. When they got to the table, he got out a pencil and a piece of paper, asking Helen for her address, which she happily wrote down for him.

As Goff started back to his table, he waved to her and heard Anne tell Helen, "Helen, I was worried about you. He kept you for so long."

"Anne, don't be silly. He's a very nice guy, and does he know how to dance, I should say. I was on air, like a feather. I was only there three or four minutes to meet his friends. They seem nice too."

"Well, he's awfully good-looking. What did you find out about him?" her curious sister asked. Anne had always wanted to know everything. Sometimes Helen thought she would end up being a cop or a newspaper reporter.

"His name is Goff Leveroos. His family has that wonderful men's store downtown. He's in the navy, twenty years old, and dances like a dream. What more could I want to know?"

"That's a good beginning. When are you going to see him again?"

"Anne, I don't know. I just met the man. Maybe soon."

"Okay. Bill, let's dance," Anne said, almost dragging him to the dance floor.

Chapter 6

The next morning Harriet and Mollie went to the Leverooses' apartment to get a few things for Betty. The landlord let them in after hearing the story and that they were taking care of Helen's little girl.

They went into the bedroom and found a little wicker bed placed beside a large adult bed. Next to the crib was a chest of drawers. Harriet opened the top drawer and found a stack of diapers, some white undershirts, three little white cotton dresses, some booties, a small hair brush, some safety pins, a rattle, a little cloth doll, and some leggings. In the second drawer she found some sheets, a baby blanket, and another doll. She put everything into a basket, which was sitting on the floor near the door. In the bathroom Mollie found baby powder and some cream, which she added to the basket. In the kitchen there were two baby bottles and nipples; she added them to the collection.

At home Mollie put the crib in the library and Betty upstairs. A moment later the baby was asleep. She ventured in every so often to check on the little girl, each time thinking how wonderful childhood is with its lack of pressure and fear or knowledge of present situations.

In the morning Mollie was awakened by Betty's crying. She didn't cry as if in distress, but as if hungry. She picked her up, cuddling and soothing her. Taking her into the kitchen, she got some milk, a sauce pan, and a towel. With Betty tucked under her arm, she explained to the child what she was doing. Last night had really been a pleasant evening, and this new little person in the house was fun and about to have her first breakfast away from home. Carefully Mollie poured the warm milk into one of the little bottles and put the nipple on. Cradling the child on her lap, she began to feed her. In just a short while the bottle was finished. She patted Betty's back, waiting for a big burp.

"There, there. Good girl. That wasn't hard, was it?" Mollie said, hugging Betty before she put her back down into the crib. She cooed back.

Chapter 7

Harriet looked over at Mollie Carey; she smiled again. Little Betty was just the ticket for this house; a new family was formed. A family, finally after years of disappointment, heartache, and desire, was now at hand. Mollie felt twenty years younger, and Frank strutted like a peacock as he carried Betty around the house, showing her each room. They began to take her everywhere, very unusual for the times, but they didn't want her to leave their sight, even for a second. Finally they began to relax with the baby, realizing she wouldn't break or run away.

That same day, Goff's mother, Sarah Erickson, sat at her dining room table, slowly composing a letter to her son.

Aug. 20, 1917

Dear Goff,

We're having fairly good weather now. The skies are so often blue with just a very few clouds. I'm watching a squirrel come down a tree stretching before he jumps off onto the ground. The Watsons still haven't painted their house, but the Smiths have. It really looks nice.

Son, I'm afraid I have some bad news, Helen left four days ago—no word, no letter, no nothing. She just up and left. I'm sorry to tell you this. I have a touch of pneumonia. Your sisters are fine. Emily is still in Chicago studying at the Art Institute, and Ebba is in Kansas seeing her friend Gloria Hunt. She should be returning next week. Hope she doesn't bring Gloria with her.

How is everything on the ship? I sure hope this war will be over soon.

Take care of yourself. Love, Mother.

Goff got the letter from his mother two weeks later. He couldn't believe what was written.

Helen gone? What? Where is Betty Gray? Why didn't Mother say? These thoughts lashed through his mind. All he could say was, "Oh my God." He kept saying it over and over.

"Hey, Goff. Bad news?" Smity Smith, second gunner, asked, seeing the strangest look on Goff's face.

"My wife is gone, my mother says."

"Oh my God. How? When?" Smith asked, wondering what it was all about.

"I don't know. My mother doesn't say. She never liked Helen," Goff almost shouted as if Smity's questions had offended him, which they had, and now Goff wanted to know what was going on, where his girls were. Helen went through his mind. She was so beautiful and womanly; even when she was pregnant she was beautiful. Her intense light-blue eyes, so full of wisdom and understanding, had brought Goff to her. She was the one who had reached in and taken his soul, gently putting it together with her own, in her heart. She wasn't a mistake like Amarelle. Amarelle was for fun, and they were young and stupid. Sex won out, and he'd run off with her when he was seventeen. He'd put her out of his mind, but he'd kept the feelings of guilt he had about her and the fact that his father had come to drag them back home then, forcing Goff to join the navy, to grow up. Now Helen was gone. How could that be? And where was Betty? Goff was stunned.

At that moment, the ship's alarm rang, piercing the air with a sharp, shrill, almost painful wailing. A moment of panic was quickly replaced with military order as each man got his gear and tried to take his battle station.

The whizzing bullets and exploding bombs—so near they shook the shoelaces on everyone's boots—filled the ship.

A barrage of bullets forced Goff and Joha to retreat to the left side of the hallway as they tried to get to their posts. All of a sudden a huge explosion threw both men to the floor, rendering them unconscious. A moment later, Joha struggled to his feet. He staggered toward Goff. His arms, side, and left leg gushed blood. The pain was so bad he wanted to die, but his buddy was in need. He could see blood pouring from the side of Goff's head. Momentarily forgetting his own problems, Joha pulled Goff up, and together they struggled to the back of the ship, collapsing on top of each other as another huge bomb hit just behind them, throwing them into the sea.

A week later they found themselves in the hospital. Neither had any idea where he was or what had happened or how they got where they were, but they were together.

"Nurse Abrahams, your patient is stirring," Nurse Williams said, briskly walking toward Joha's bed. Jane Abrahams had enlisted six days before the big push and was assigned to this detail because she was the best in her class for work with trauma cases. It was terrible work, so much pain and suffering to deal with, but she had what it took. The blood, it was everywhere, and the crying screams of the poor boys whose blood drenched the operating room would resonate in her brain forever, but Nurse Abrahams's fortitude brought order. She was tough, almost like a man, but also gentle and sometimes overly sentimental, sighing with unabated desire as she watched wrenching movie scenes of Rudolph Valentino's sheik dancing the tango with Helena Domingues.

Joha's injuries took over several months to heal as did Goff's, leaving him partially deaf and Joha with scars he would have for the rest of his life, making for good antiwar stories down the line. When the war finally ended, each man went his own way. Goff often thought of Joha's heroism and friendship, realizing they did not let life just occur. Such friends he knew were only for the moment, that short second in history when friendships were formed. Nowadays Joha was only a memory, but one Goff knew he would take to his grave.

Lying in bed, Goff had time to think. Thoughts seemed to rush at him, making him wonder if what he remembered or thought he did was true. Had he gotten a letter from his mother telling him his wife and daughter had left? Each day brought a terrible fear that this was probably the case; if only that letter hadn't been lost in the chaos of the bombing. Now he wasn't sure about anything, except somehow he had survived.

September 10 came in with more rain than Goff had ever seen. It poured down as though the gods were angry. Slowly his wounds were healing as were Joha's. Today they would be invalided out of the navy and homeward bound. Joha to Milwaukee and Goff to St. Paul.

Boarding the ship on stretchers, the two men were put in the ship's infirmary. Ten days later they disembarked in New York, each going his separate way as Helen proceeded to Hollywood, feeling satisfied that Betty was in good hands.

Chapter 8

Upon his arrival back to St. Paul, Goff found his apartment empty, as his mother had written—no wife, no daughter. As he stood in the entranceway, he saw everything was in its proper place. He could feel a weird kind of quiet. *Where were they? Where was Helen? What had she done with Betty?* he wondered. Everything looked the same, untouched, except the heart of the place was missing. The quiet seemed to be more pronounced as he went into the living room. This had been the room where their life had been lived. Helen had rocked Betty in the antique wooden rocking chair they got from her uncle; they played cards at the small tea table in front of the couch; he paid the bills at that table and did the crossword puzzle there. Even the bathroom, with its white and black tiles on the floor and the big bathtub and sink, seemed lacking life.

"My mother!" He turned, going toward the door. He decided she would have some answers, at least he hoped.

It took him half an hour to walk to his mother's. She was just about to have lunch as he rang her bell.

"Son. I'm so happy to see you," she said, embracing him. "Take off your coat. Come, sit down in the dining room. I'll get the soup. We'll have lunch. Are you hungry? I'm starved." She directed him as if he'd just come in from a day at school.

"Mother, when I got to the apartment Helen wasn't there nor Betty. Where are they?"

She didn't answer him as she went into the kitchen to bring the tomato soup. She brought it out and put the bowls of warming soup in front of their regular places.

He asked again, "Where are Helen and Betty?"

"I don't know," was all she could say.

During lunch Sarah Leveroos did everything in her power not to mention Helen or Betty. When they'd finished she handed her son a long white envelope with the name Fischer, Havoc & Douglas printed in the upper left corner. It had arrived some three months earlier.

"What's this?" he asked

"I don't know, but I think you need to take care of it," she said. "Looks important."

"Your tone tells me you know." He looked at her.

"I can guess," the older lady said, looking back at him as she turned to go back into the kitchen to do the dishes, not wanting to become involved with whatever it was she suspected Helen had done. This would be just one more thing to add to the long list of things Helen had done that Sarah felt showed her selfish, indulgent ways. How had Goff gotten involved with her, she didn't know; and why, oh why had he married her? Of all the girls in St. Paul or Minneapolis or the whole country, why her? Sarah Leveroos was a strong woman who had endured, as she thought of it, a husband and three high-spirited children, all of whom she felt had given her little peace or comfort for all the years of trying to take care of them properly. Helen was at least, she thought, better than that Annabelle, who one morning came out of Goff's bedroom announcing that she was the new Mrs. Leveroos and things around the place were going to change. That sixteen-year-old girl, and her ideas of change, lasted about a week before Goff's father took him to talk to a judge. They quickly obtained an annulment of the marriage. This wasn't the case for Helen; she was a permanent part of the household. Sarah had tried to like Helen, but there was too much of a contrast between them. Sarah wanted her to help around the house, but Helen had little idea of household management: cooking, cleaning, ironing, or, as Sarah felt, how to take care of Betty. Sarah also thought she was too self-indulgent, spending money recklessly on clothes and things for herself. Adding to Sarah's dislike, she thought Helen was secretive because she never told her anything about what she did at the theater the nights she was there.

Goff quickly opened the legal-sized envelope. Pulling the document out, he found it to be a divorce decree. The reason: nonsupport. He cried.

By the time Goff arrived home, Helen had gotten a good role in a Rudolph Valentino film, and by the time the film was released their divorce had been finalized. Goff was angered that the grounds submitted by her attorney had been for nonsupport. He didn't want anyone to ever believe he didn't take care of Betty or her. That's one reason he'd gone to war—to protect them and the country, not to abandon them. He had no idea Helen had given Betty to Harriet and that Harriet had arranged for her to go to the Careys. He saw he'd never really known how Helen thought. He thought she seemed to love him and he was happy. He also had no idea Helen's lawyer had said that if she wanted Hollywood the only way was to give Betty to Harriet. She wanted her freedom. As the years went on, so did Helen's career. Two films a year, sometimes three, kept her from thinking of getting Betty back or that she would be adopted by the Careys. By the time Helen had finished film number eleven, she was already twenty-eight and Betty was in the sixth grade. By the time Betty was a freshman in high school, Helen had an impressive resume of twenty-five films to her credit. As each film debuted, Betty continued to grow into a sweet young lady, enjoying the luxurious life required for the beginning of a young debutante.

This is what Mollie wanted, plus all the finery that could be had through Frank's work. They had fun. They loved the big house on Lake of the Isles Boulevard, the parties given there, those wonderful carefree days spent on their yacht, *Peggy*, sailing the eastern coast of Florida and back, and special friendships with some of America's most influential people. They loved seeing their daughter had a way about her that led her to take things in stride, and they were happy to let Betty experience everything there was. It was all part of the good life.

Betty, to their great surprise, was very good at sports, having a deep love for horses. She seemed to be born with an aptitude for the equestrian challenge, winning enough ribbons to fill a small suitcase and enough trophies to add a lovely silver essence to the shelves of the library by the end of her equestrian career. Granted there were some falls that scared Mollie, making her talk to her daughter about the dangers of all this, but she never told her to stop. As a result Betty suffered a broken arm, incurred several deep cuts when the horses got too close together, and was stepped on several times by a thousand-pound horse; but she endured all of them without a word of quitting. Betty also had a fine academic mind, especially for literature and poetry. She loved to write about her horses and things young girls wonder about, such as sleep, the dark, or where the wind comes from. One of Mollie's favorites was "To the Wind."

The wind is a woman,
Queen of all the elements!
Hear her skirt brush
Against the upstretched arms
Of the welcoming trees
As she rides on high!
Hear them rustling, murmuring, whispering,
As they bow down
Before her gentle caresses.

Ah! She has touched my cheek . . .
And is gone.

Another Mollie loved was "In Praise of Dan Patch," which was to be sung to the tune of "Louise," made famous by Maurice Chevalier.

Helen quietly kept up with Betty's achievements as various films and their premiers took her around the country. Glorious newspaper praise, some even suggesting Betty was a possible Olympic contender, was handed out in Chicago, Minneapolis, Milwaukee, Indiana, and Iowa. Helen often picked up a newspaper to read a small headline about Betty Carey winning this prize or that trophy, presented by this club or that club. Beaming with internal pride, she'd carefully clip the article out and put it in a special box she'd made with the initial *B* pasted on its dark-blue velvet cover.

Chapter 9

For Helen, the worrisome thing was, as the number of films she'd been in increased, so did her age. Now at age thirty-five, she began to hear gossip about her ageing. People, especially directors, seemed to treat her differently. Instead of giving her the main role, they began to offer bit parts and those of old, scruffy women. The last film she did in Hollywood, she played a corpse and was covered by a white sheet throughout the scene while the newest starlet acted around her. She didn't even get credit when they were shown at the end of the film. To add insult to injury, the people around seemed to change; familiar faces were gone, and in their place were a lot of young, vain, pompous, airheads who didn't know or remember her. Not only that, but the morals of the day had also changed. Granted sex had always been a part of things, but now drugs came into the picture, and more and more of these poor, stupid, young people seemed to be ruled by both, thinking this was the way to get the good part. It was quite enough! It was time for her to continue her life elsewhere. She'd heard wonderful films were being made in Austria now; this cast the die.

Chapter 10

In 1934 a major tragedy struck the Carey household when Frank unexpectedly died. The weather had been cool with a light rain forecasted for that day. Before he left the house, Mollie had told him to get a sweater for underneath his coat, but he was in a hurry and didn't. Getting into the car, he gingerly tossed the coat into the backseat. By the time he arrived at his office, a gentle, light rain was falling. He parked and got out of his Packard, not even looking for the coat or remembering what Mollie had said about the weather.

It was going to be a full day—meetings with the Board of Trade officials, who came specifically to Minneapolis to see him to discuss some ideas on how to deal with the dying crops resulting from the drought in the West and Midwest. They also wanted his thoughts on the latest figures of the number of cattle being shipped from Texas to Chicago from the last quarter. Even before he'd become its president, the Chicago Board of Trade had been one of Frank's favorite buildings—elegantly strong looking, standing tall at the end of La Salle Street, wearing its mantle of light gray, giving a sense of assurance. He sometimes thought of this building as a lady who knew who she was. He had a lot of respect for everything that went on inside those gray walls. It was there the country grew, both financially and prestigiously, while the whole world looked to see every day what happened inside. He was delighted when the fellows from within these beautiful walls came to see him, but the best part of the day would be at three thirty when a meeting with his friend Herbert Hoover had been arranged. Frank had wonderful memories of the challenging time they spent working so hard to deed Europe after WWI. He wondered what his old colleague had up his sleeve.

At three thirty, on the dot, Herbert Hoover was announced by Frank's secretary, Janet. With a hardy handshake, they sat down to talk. By six thirty it was time for dinner, and they were both hungry. Dayton's was close, but so was a little steak joint they both liked just across the street. They decided the steak joint would ease the pressure of the day's work away along with a couple of good drinks. They wondered what it was about beef and booze that could transform a weary man into a champion within an hour.

As they walked out the office door, Janet handed Frank a note she'd written earlier during the meeting, telling him the city needed to block off the street and had reparked his car six blocks up using the spare set of keys Janet had in her desk.

"Look at this, would you?" Frank said, handing the note to Mr. Hoover.

"Wouldn't you know!" he said, reading it as they walked out toward the restaurant. "What next? Well, what can I do?" he asked, throwing his hands up.

A moment later they sat down to the warm and friendly atmosphere of the steak house and a happy waitress, who told them she had four daughters and seven grandchildren. They were amazed, thinking she was only about forty years old. Good food and stories from the war days and family filled the evening. Herbert had even remembered the menu Mollie had served him and his wife Lou the last time they came to dinner, saying, kind of dreamily, it was the best chocolate pie he'd ever eaten. After dinner they both had a brandy and a little more talk about the present political situation, of which they were both worried, the Board of Trade, and their wives. Then each went to find his own bed with fond farewells to each other as they parted company, sending greetings to the other's wife.

It was raining as Frank got to the restaurant's door. Now he wished he'd brought his coat. He picked up a newspaper, which was sitting on a small table near the door, to cover his head.

A cool wind had begun to blow, not too strong but enough to agitate the tree branches and to lightly throw some small pieces of paper along the street. As he stepped onto the sidewalk, he could feel the wind pushing against him and the rains' coldness against the back of his neck, face, and hands. They seemed to work like a menacing team, but he was a tough Irishman. A little wind and rain wouldn't hurt him.

As he quickly walked along, each block seemed to get longer and longer. It also began raining harder. Now the newspaper head cover began to wither, almost disintegrate, as his steps brought him closer to his car.

"Thank God, only one more block to go," he said out loud. "But I don't see my car ahead. Where could that idiot have put it?" Looking forward between the sheeting rain, he finally spotted it on the other side of the street. *Thank heaven*, he thought as he pulled the keys out of his pocket, opened the door, and almost collapsed into the driver's seat. He was wet to the skin, breathing a little heavier and shivering by now. How lovely the interior of his new navy-blue Packard seemed at that moment.

He was so happy to put the key into the ignition and start the trip home; in twenty minutes he'd be there. It was eleven by the time he drove into the driveway. He could feel a slight headache, and he was chilled, a kind of cold he'd never felt before, making his teeth chatter. As he got out of the car, his body ached. He was never so glad to see Mollie as she opened the door to him.

"Darling, I was worried. It's eleven o'clock. Where have you been?" she asked as she helped him out of his wet jacket.

"I had dinner with Herbert Hoover. Because of the weather we had dinner at that little steak place across from the office. Can you imagine, during dinner the city moved my car so I had to walk several blocks to find it. Oh, he sends many greetings to you," he told her, shivering.

"Thank you for his greetings. I'd forgotten you were going to see him today. I'm sorry you had such a problem with the car. How's Lou?"

"She's fine. God, my head aches."

"Darling, come upstairs. I'm going to draw you a nice warm bath. I'll put your pajamas, robe, and slippers in the bathroom. Now take off those wet things. I'll take care of them." She gently directed him.

Within fifteen minutes, Frank lowered himself into the warm water the tub offered. He could hear Betty wishing him a good night from the other side of the door. All of a sudden he felt happy his daughter cared so much for him and he for her. He loved her deeply.

"The same to you, my little girl," he answered back, splashing the water gently over his chest. It felt so good.

He sat there letting the warmth of the water revive him. Feeling a little better, he slowly raised himself out of the tub, but as he did he could feel the headache starting to strengthen. Taking a towel from the towel bar, he quickly dried himself and then put on his pajamas. Catching a glimpse of himself in the medicine cabinet mirror, he saw an old, tired-looking man. Was that really him? He couldn't believe how tired he looked when that same morning he was raring to go—such a change, so quickly. He opened the bathroom door and headed toward the bedroom. Entering this pleasant and happy room, he flopped down on the bed, pulled up the covers, and quietly laid there. He began to shiver again.

"Mollie, would you bring me another blanket?" he called out. "I'm very cold."

Going down the hall, she took two heavy blankets from the linen closet, brought them in the room, and put them on top of Frank, who was by now beginning to wheeze strongly.

"I don't like this. I'm calling Dr. Cohn," she told him.

"All right, might be a good idea," he agreed. When she heard him agree, her worry increased.

At that she went downstairs to look up the doctor's phone number. Telling him Frank's symptoms, the doctor said he'd be there as soon as possible. She then went to make a cup of tea for Frank. Taking it to him, she found him shaking and burning up at the same time. Taking his temperature, the thermometer told her he had a fever of 103. She helped him take a couple of sips of the hot tea and then went downstairs when she heard the doctor knock on the door.

"Good evening, Mrs. Carey," Dr. Cohen said. "Where is he?"

"He's upstairs in bed. I'll show you. He's got a temperature of one hundred three. When I brought some tea to him a moment ago he was shaking. Walking around town in cold rain is not good for older people."

"Why was he out in the rain?"

"The city reparked his car."

"Oh, what next?" he stated angrily.

Entering the room, he could see Frank shaking under the blankets and that he was very pale. After a good examination he gave him a couple of aspirins and some quinine, telling him to repeat this every four hours, to drink lots of hot liquids, to stay in bed, and not to worry about the world, that it would take care of itself. Frank thanked him for coming. As Mollie walked him to the door, she asked his opinion.

"Mollie, he's got to stay in bed. His lungs don't sound all that bad, but we'll see how things are in the morning. Just keep an eye on him."

"All right. Will you come again in the morning?"

"I can stop on my way to the office. Don't worry, he's tough. Now you need to get some rest too."

"Thank you. I will. See you tomorrow. Good night."

"Good night. Call me if things change."

"I will." Mollie watched him walk to his car. She shut the door and then went into the kitchen to make more tea for both of them. When she got upstairs she found him asleep. Putting the tea down on the bedside table, she went to get undressed. It was tepid by the time she got back. A cup of tepid tea in hand, she sat down in the overstuffed bedroom chair and just watched him sleep. Usually she went to bed first, so this opportunity was unique. By ten all the Careys were in bed.

As the night progressed, Mollie could hear Frank's restlessness. He seemed to nervously toss and turn. She could hear that his breathing became heavy, but he didn't seem to be in pain, other than the headache he complained of when he came home. She got up once to put another blanket on him and to give him another aspirin. Finally he settled down a little. She got back into bed and laid there listening to her husband. Around five in the morning, she heard him give out a little gasp. He was quiet until she got up at seven thirty.

"How are you this morning, darling?" she asked. "Feeling better?" He didn't answer. She looked over at him. He was unusually quiet.

Something was very wrong.

"Frank. Frank! Oh my God!" she said, panic in her voice. "Frank!" Leaping up, she ran to the telephone, calling Dr. Cohen and waking Betty in the process.

"I think Frank is dead. Please come immediately."

"Mother. What's happening?" Betty asked, running in to see her mother.

"It's your father. I'm talking to Dr. Cohen now. Would you go downstairs and wait for him."

"Yes. Right away. Is Daddy all right?"

"I don't know. Please go wait for the doctor."

"Okay, Mother." Betty said, sensing something bad, something beyond her, out of her reach, was starting to stir up the household.

As she waited for Dr. Cohen, a fear of loss also came, throwing itself over her. She started to softly cry. She loved her father so. He was the core of their life, home, everything. She never thought there could be a time without him. She had just assumed he would be around forever. Now that was being pushed to the side, replaced by the reality of life. There was nothing she could do but wait. Finally Dr. Cohen arrived, tearing into the house. He dashed upstairs to Mollie, who'd heard him come in. Betty closely followed behind. He quickly asked her again what she knew. Then looking down where Frank lay, he could tell he was dead.

"I'm sorry, Mrs. Carey. He's gone," the doctor said, looking at her with true pity in his eyes. He liked Frank. He'd been an easy and grateful patient.

These words struck Betty like jagged lightning. She gasped. Mollie pulled her close, and they hugged each other tightly. They both cried as Dr. Cohen covered Frank. He then went over to Mollie and Betty again, saying he was sorry.

Finally collecting herself enough to get the words out, she said, "Thank you. What now?"

"I'll have the funeral parlor come for him. Which one do you want to work with?" he asked, offering his handkerchief to her. Taking it, she wiped her eyes and handed it back to him.

"I don't know. What do you recommend?"

"There are several good ones."

"How can a man who was so much alive thirty hours ago be dead so quickly?"

"It's a difficult question, one that most likely needs a scientific explanation. We can conduct an autopsy if you like."

"No. I don't want him cut up! No," she sharply responded. That's fine," he answered.

Four days later Frank's sudden death and now his funeral put Mollie in a strange daze; she somehow seemed to be there but was not. The sudden flood of attention threw her off course. There were so many people around, faces from the past she hadn't seen in years and faces from just yesterday, all mingling around seeming to ask the same questions. She wondered when it would end. Thank heaven Betty, at her tender age, was like the Rock Of Gibraltar for Mollie. She marveled at Betty's ability to cope and manage so well and so intelligently help in so many of the decisions that had to be so quickly made.

The funeral was a glorious tribute to a man who deserved to be remembered, as the minister said. A man who had done more good than bad in his life, a man people admired and respected for the things he'd accomplished, for his generosity, his honest work ethic in business, his work after the war, and his love for his wife and child.

Finally at 3:00 p.m., Mollie and Betty drove away from Sunset Memorial Cemetery. They were glad to arrive home, but it was hard to go into the house knowing Frank wasn't there. The spirit of the house had changed, leaving a feeling of emptiness, which permeated everything.

Mollie wearily took off her coat, sank down onto the couch, and started to weep.

"Why? Why? Why?" She slowly sobbed over and over again. "How could this be?"

"Oh, Mother. I wish I knew," Betty answered, her tears returning. She went over to Mollie, sat down beside her, and put her arms around her, needing her mother's loving caress.

"Thank you, sweet girl. You're my life," Mollie said. Her tears had finally stopped, and a slight smile came to her face as she realized, for the umpteenth time, how much she loved Betty and how lucky she'd been to have gotten this child. Looking over at Betty, she put her hands on her face and kissed her repeatedly, telling her again how much she was loved and that she was wonderful.

"I love you too. I'm feeling tired. I'm going to lie down for a while.

Let's go upstairs and rest together."

"Yes, let's," Mollie agreed. Going into her bedroom, Mollie slipped off her shoes, lying down on the bed she'd shared with Frank. She could smell him. His special aftershave made her, for that second, feel happy, remembering so many wonderful nights they'd lain in that fine bed with it's luxurious bedding and fine pillows. Tapping the area beside her, Betty came to join her mother. Mollie put her arm around Betty as she snuggled beside her. Within a moment, they were both asleep.

Chapter 11

It took a long time for Mollie to recover and to come back to a normal but different regimen. Frank's death left the house so different; everything seemed to lack luster; even the streetlights seemed paler and, in a sense, useless. Finally she seemed to have a new attitude. The grief they both felt seemed less, and Mollie saw the streetlights in the old way again.

The hardest part for her in this was Betty's grief. Every night, lying in bed alone across the hall, she would listen to Betty sobbing for her father. She began to wonder if they'd been too close. Why did love hurt so much? The perfect threesome was now a twosome, and the void it formed made both Mollie and Betty long for better days.

As the days slipped into weeks, and weeks into months, things eased. Summer was at hand; it was time to put the pieces of the Carey household back in proper order. A party, Betty suggested, was the answer. Her father loved parties, and so did she; it had always been the norm.

"Darling, what a good idea. We've been like two bumps on a log for too long," her mother agreed

"We need this. Let's make a long guest list, lots of people. I'd like to invite some of my new friends from school."

"That's a good idea, young people," she said, continuing in a newly found happy tone of voice.

"I'm even going to include father's business partners and their wives. You haven't seen Mrs. Hallet for such a long time."

They both smiled; this was the right thing. One month later, 6:00 p.m., Friday the sixteenth; the house was ready.

The dining room table was artistically arranged, as only Mrs. Carter could do. Her catering service only sparingly given to those she considered the upper crust of society. She'd placed two silver trays, one at each end, one containing a whole poached salmon ringed by thin tomato wedges and topped with chopped aspic, which shimmered like golden jewels in the light. Bowls of poached shrimp with cocktail sauce; liver paté with toast points; herbed mayonnaise dip and freshly cut carrot strips, green pepper strips, cauliflower florets, and sliced mushrooms; rare roast beef surrounded by a light, creamy horseradish sauce; and a chafing dish filled with beef Stroganoff made using cream cheese all stood in scattered rows waiting to be consumed. This last recipe was given by Harriet, and huge platters of frosted sugar cookies. A bartender named Simon and two women to serve drinks and tend tables were hired.

The lighting was low, almost romantic, throughout the house; a feeling of happy pleasure was more and more pronounced as the guests arrived. A special spotlight lit Frank's official portrait from the Chicago Board of Trade, which hung above the fireplace in the living room. The house hadn't had such spirit for a long time it felt right. Mollie looked beautiful. Her hair, more than starting to gray, shined silvery in the lighting of each room. The long light-blue, sequined dress with its suggestive décolleté and long shawl of white chiffon, covered in matching sequins and applique pansies, draped her shoulders in an almost seductive manner. Her perfume was Frank's favorite, Shalimar. She chose her mother's diamond necklace and a large diamond cocktail ring, which added its own shimmer.

Betty, equally elegant, came out in a long dark-green velvet dress. A three-strand crystal bead necklace and her mother's diamond watch were all the jewelry she needed. Her medium-brown hair, freshly washed and curled, shined in the lighting of the night.

"How do I look? Not too flamboyant for a newly widowed woman, I hope," Mollie asked Betty, looking at her daughter. She loved her more than ever for the strength, kindness, and caring she has always shown her family. She couldn't have gotten through the past dark days without her wonderful girl. Their roles had become reversed; now Betty seemed to be the mother, the hand that directed her mother gently out of the heartbreak of her husband's death.

"You look wonderful. The dress is so pretty, and Grandma Whittich's necklace is lovely."

"Thank you. You also look so elegant. Your father would be so proud of you. I think I hear someone at the door. Let's go see about it," Mollie said, wiping her eye, not letting a little tear form. Together they opened the door to the party's first guests: Mr. and Mrs. Hallet.

"Cynthia, how lovely to see you. You look wonderful," Mollie greeted the older lady. "And, Ed. Please come in. We have a bar set up in the living room in front of the fireplace. I've set up a buffet in the dining room. Enjoy."

Cynthia Hallet was a fashion icon. Having a fabulous sense of style, she bought and could afford the best clothing, shoes, and jewelry Minneapolis had to offer. Her favorite treasure for these things was Strem's Fashion Studio on Nicollet Avenue. Tonight, dressed in a tangerine brocade two-piece dress with a matching shawl, her signature three-strand pearl necklace, and large matching baroque pearl ring, she set the fashion scene once again.

Cynthia had a special feeling toward Mollie, almost sisterlike. She enjoyed her company, her fun way of thinking and her style. She was always amazed at Mollie's sense of spontaneity and adventure, sometimes leading them into laughable situations. She especially liked the parties Mollie and Frank gave. It would be different, now that Frank had passed, but she'd always be close; that wouldn't change.

"Mollie," Ed said, looking at her as if for the first time. "This is quite an evening. Thank heaven it's now too hot yet. The house looks the same. I'm glad you haven't changed things." He was smiling at her, adding, "You look beautiful."

"Thank you, Ed."

At that, four more couples arrived, bringing the noise level up dramatically. Simon was immediately busied making the newest cocktails; the two women servers seemed to hand out drinks faster than they could keep up with.

"Blanche, did you try the salmon?" Gert Stewart asked Blanche Campbell. "It's supreme. Of course, everything Mollie does is wonderful."

"I'm just headed over there now. I heard Sylvia Durham say the roast beef was good too—not surprising."

The husbands of these two cousins, also distant cousins, had worked with Frank since day one when the president had asked them to start work on the program to feed Europe after World War I. It had been a complicated process, never done on such a scale before. The war had done havoc as never seen before, and Europe had been in dire straits. US boys, as they called themselves, had finally gotten enough food into the hand of the hungry masses to bring them out of despair. Europe slowly got back on its feet, a process that needed a great deal of patience and unity from the winning side.

One of the last to arrive was Arnie Devon. Arnie, a widower for five years, lived across the street. He'd casually known Frank through the annual neighborhood party given every August. They'd worked on the board of directors of the Evergreen Corp. Mollie knew Arnie's wife, Joanne, through her membership in the women's bridge club, and Betty shared classes with their daughter Alice at the University of Minnesota. It wasn't a friendship as with the Hallets; it was only continued for business purposes. Mollie never thought of either of them very much. They were kind of like the big trees across the street—there. Frank really wasn't interested in them even though a friendship could have been formed; he never invited Arnie over for a drink after the board meetings, never suggested they go out together, and never played golf with him. Even with all the things that brought them together, nothing did.

The doorbell rang again. This time it was Betty's friend Summer Powell, who'd brought a very handsome friend.

"Summer, I'm glad you could come," Betty said, eyeing the good-looking young man Summer had at her side.

"Betty, this is Kevin MacArthur. He's in theater. Right now he's rehearsing for Eugene O'Neill's *Beyond the Horizon*. My, you look pretty. How's your mother? Mine sends many regards. I've been so looking forward to this party. Oh, there's your mother. I must go over to say hello." Summer chattered away, not seeing at all the effect Kevin MacArthur was having on Betty—not that Summer and Kevin were dating or anything. They're just study buddies, as Kevin had said, which suited Summer just fine.

"Hello. Welcome." Betty looked straight at Kevin as he offered his hand.

He looked back, saying, "Thank you." He liked her look. He sensed she knew a thing or two. He'd had his fill of empty-headed females. The last one, Linda Lees, repeatedly embarrassed him when they were out or with friends with her unknowing answers when asked even the simplest question about nearly everything. He was glad Jim Smith, left guard on the Minnesota state basketball team, stole her away. Now he was free to concentrate on class and the new play's rehearsal schedule and open for proper conversation. "I'm happy to meet you. This is such a beautiful house. Are you studying at the university?" he asked, just looking at her; quietly she'd captured his full attention. Kevin wasn't the type to go gaga over every girl. He had to know them somewhat before some sort of feeling came, but Betty was different—pretty and gentle with a warm, open smile, which just brought her to him.

"I'm happy to meet you too. I am at the university, studying like mad, like everyone else," she said, taking his hand.

"Me too."

"What classes are you taking?" she asked, wondering if they would ever been in any classes together.

"I'm taking theater history, acting, geology, Italian, and math, And you?" he answered "That's a pretty full load. I'm taking English lit, American history, geometry, French 1, and chemistry."

"We're both pretty booked up." He sort of laughed.

"What do you like best?" she asked, feeling he was almost too good-looking to be so smart.

"Defiantly theater, acting. I love it. I want to be a professional actor."

"Really." Betty was surprised. She thought men were supposed to do steady, sturdy, or solid things. Acting didn't seem to fit him, or maybe it did. In any case, she felt he looked more like a lawyer.

"Yes. Acting has always been in the Irish blood," he said just as Mollie walked by, hearing him add, "I'm Irish. There is just something about acting that makes me happy. To make a scene or play real, to make a character come to life and to have an audience respond to that makes me feel I've accomplished something, and it's fun.".

"Oh. I guess I can see it might be fun. It does sound interesting. I like to write poetry. You've given me an incentive to write one about an actor." Betty smiled.

"I hope you will. I'm in a new show. I hope you and your mother will come to see it. It opens in three weeks at the University Theater. It's a great Eugene O'Neill piece."

"I'd love to. I'll be there," Betty said, smiling. Continuing, she changed the subject. "It's been hard getting Mother to do things since my father recently died. A night at the theater might just be the thing."

"I'm sorry about your father. How are you and your mother coping?" he asked, his twinkling blue eyes graying a little with concern.

"It's been very hard. Mother's finally beginning to come out of it."

"That's good. I remember how hard it was for me when my grandparents died. If I can do anything to help," he quickly said, remembering back on those times. Those black times without his grandfather's support and affection were awful; he understood

"That's very nice of you, but we're much better now," she said, adding, "Kevin, to come back to a happier theme, we've got a very nice buffet table set up in the dining room. The bar is over there in the living room. Are you hungry?" Betty asked, pointing to the right.

"I must say I am," he smiled at the anticipation of something to eat. He hadn't had anything since breakfast but the quick cup of coffee after rehearsal this afternoon. He was really ready for something good.

Just as Kevin started toward the dining room, the three-piece combo Mollie hired finally made their entrance. They started with a five-minute warm-up leading into "After the Ball." Kevin quickly looked over the table, deciding he wanted some of the salmon and some of the paté. Putting them and several toast points on his plate, he stood beside the table watching Betty dance with an older man. She seemed to glide to the music with an elegance he'd never seen. They really looked good together. Finishing up the food on his plate, he headed toward her and saw Summer in a deep conversation with a very tall girl. As the next number, "Tea for Two," began the older man led Betty back to the floor; but a moment later Kevin cut in, gently tapping him on the shoulder.

"May I cut in?" he asked the older fellow.

"By all means."

"Betty, would you like to dance?" he asked, leading her into his arms. "Yes," was all she could say. It had been hard to tell him of her father's death, but the invitation to dance from this gorgeous man just made her happy. "Tea for Two" and Kevin MacArthur took her away from the remembrance of death and all that it had taken from her.

Kevin's style of dancing impressed Betty; his rhythm, timing, and sense of beat to "Tea for Two" kept her feeling as though they'd always danced together. He didn't make her feel dragged along like a dog on a leash but guided.

"Have you known Summer long?" he asked, feeling the softness of her dress on his hand as he held her waist.

"We've been friends since high school. She's a great gal. How long have you known her?" Betty asked.

"We just met about two or three months ago. I met her while waiting in line at the school cafeteria," Kevin answered, starting a turn, releasing Betty then gently pulling her back. There was something nice about the way she danced; it was so natural.

"Have you been dating her since then?" Betty nervously asked.

"Well, actually we don't date like most people think. If I need a date I ask her, and if she can, she does, and vice versa."

"Now that is interesting."

"Not really. We've just been so busy there isn't time for it."

"That's also interesting."

"I don't think it is that interesting. She's my friend, not my girlfriend," he said, leading her into another turn. Betty smiled.

"I understand. Sometimes school is so overpowering."

"I feel the same. Maybe I should study less and date more."

"I wish I could, I mean date more, if I had someone to date."

"You don't have a steady boyfriend?" He was shocked. She was such a great-looking girl, and smart; he couldn't understand it.

"Not at the moment," she confessed. Now he smiled.

"Could I take you to dinner next Saturday?"

"I'd like that," she said, smiling again, wondering if it showed on her face how much she liked him.

Mollie watched as Betty began to dance with Kevin. She could see Betty's ease on the dance floor and wondered where it came from. She could hear her dress swish as she waltzed by, but she felt something was amiss about them. Arnie then came up beside her, took her hand, enticing her to the floor. It felt odd not to be dancing with Frank, but Arnie glided her into the one-two-three beat, making her momentarily forget she wasn't with Frank. He held her fast, and his near perfect rhythm made her feel she was gently flying. It was fun, a kind of fun she hadn't had in a long time, making her feel she shouldn't be enjoying the dance quite so much. Mollie was almost out of breath when they finally got back to the table. "My goodness! I haven't danced like that for a long time. I'm surprised I still can." Mollie sort of laughed at herself when it was finished.

"It's good for you. You moved like a gazelle," he said, seating her. "Would you like a glass of champagne?"

"Yes. That would be very nice." As she watched him leave for the bar, she felt as though life was all of a sudden moving too fast. Frank's death, Betty being home, daily life, and this party all seemed to be upon her. She didn't seem to have enough time to absorb one thing before another came. She needed time; it was just the way she was.

When the next song finished, Betty brought Kevin over to say hello.

"Mother, I'd like for you to meet Kevin MacArthur. He's also at the university. He's here with Summer."

"Good evening, Mrs. Carey," Kevin said, extending his hand.

"Good evening." She took his hand, thinking, at the same time, what a positively handsome fellow he was.

Arnie then arrived with two glasses of champagne. While handing one to Mollie, he looked over at Betty and Kevin. Doing so, he bumped his hand against another man who, just at that moment, happened to walk by. Most of the champagne spilled directly on Mollie's bodice and shawl. She looked down at her wet dress in horror.

"Arnie, agh!" she said with disbelief.

Seeming totally unaware of the situation or any concern for her, he started introducing himself. "Hello. I'm Arnie Devon. I'm Alice's father," he said, looking at them.

Looking straight at him, Betty coldly said, "Good evening." Turning to her mother, she calmly added, "Mother, let me get something to dry your dress right away." She didn't like this incredibly rude manner. How dare he not offer a word of apology. Certainly he saw what had happened. "Let's go to the ladies' room. Kevin, please introduce yourself. I'll be right back."

Betty gently took Mollie's arm, turning her toward the ladies' room. "What a strange thing to happen. My, I really am soaked," she said with disbelief.

Betty took several of the terry cloth hand towels stacked in two neat piles beside the sink, gently but firmly drying her mother's sleeve.

"It's getting better. I'm able to get a lot of it, but I'd like to get you home and into something dry. Are you warm enough?"

"Betty, dear, it's all right. I don't want to make a scene about it or for you to be upset. I'm fine. You do such a wonderful job of taking care of me. Thank you, darling," Mollie said, giving Betty a kiss on her cheek.

"I always will, Mother," Betty said.

"What's that terribly handsome man's name again?" Mollie asked, dabbing her arm, wanting to hear if it was an Irish name, as she had thought.

"Kevin MacArthur. He is a dish, isn't he!" Betty said, smiling.

"Very much so." Mollie smiled, agreeing and then giving the wet towel to Betty to put in the hamper beside the sink.

Kevin, waiting for Betty to return, introduced himself to Arnie, mentioning he had several classes with her.

Arnie also noticed Kevin was a very good-looking man, and this let a thought of how he might be a good choice for his daughter enter his mind. He introduced himself. "My daughter Alice is also at the U. Have you met her?"

"I don't think so. What's she studying?" he asked, looking at the, he thought, aggressive and callous man.

"A little of this and that. I want her to have a well-rounded education."

"Oh, I don't think I've met her. Alice Devon—no, the name isn't familiar," Kevin said, thinking. He really had never heard of her.

"Too bad. She's such a great girl and beautiful. You two might make a great team."

Kevin, not knowing what to say at this, offered, "It's a wonderful party. I'm looking forward to the buffet table." Just at that second, Summer happily joined him after a very long conversation with an old friend she hadn't seen in years.

"Summer. Hi. This is Arnie Devon. His daughter Alice is also at the U. Do you know her? Summer is my date," Kevin said in a voice he hoped told Arnie he wasn't free.

"Hi. Hello. Alice Devon?" Summer said the name again. "No. I'm afraid she's not in any of my classes."

"Oh, too bad," Arnie said, looking toward the bar, his voice dropping.

"Summer, let's see what the buffet table has to offer," Kevin said while kind of pulling her arm to get away from the man.

"Good idea. I'm hungry."

Arnie turned toward the bar.

As Kevin brought Summer to the table, they met Mollie and Betty while they were enjoying some of the shrimp. Summer's eyes opened wide at the fabulous abundance of food on the table. She'd never seen such food, such elegant food, and so much of it in one place.

"Mrs. Carey, what a beautiful table you've set. I'm very pleased to see you and Betty again. How are you?" Summer said, not realizing the incident of a moment ago.

"I'm just fine, dear. Thank you. Are you enjoying yourself?" Mollie sweetly asked. She didn't know Summer well but liked her from the first time Betty brought her home about six months ago. She also liked Summer's parents. Ellen and Bill were good people, giving all of themselves to their daughters Summer and Spring.

"Hi, Betty. I just had such a wonderful chat with Dora Jones. I haven't seen her in the longest time. I was so surprised and happy to see her. Do you remember her?" Summer told Mollie, smiling at Betty, who warmly smiled back and nodded yes.

"I'm very glad." Mollie smiled, adding, "Do try some of the salmon.

It's Mrs. Carter's specialty, and her paté is very good today."

"Thank you, I will. May I get some for you?" Summer offered.

"No, thank you, dear. I'll eat later," Mollie said, looking at Summer's dress, thinking how well she looked in green.

"Betty, are you free for lunch one day next week?" Summer asked, looking at Betty, realizing it had been months since they had spent any time together.

"I'm sure so," Betty said, also realizing it had been a long time. "Please call me."

"I will," she answered.

As Mollie talked to Summer, Betty's mind was filled with the blatant fact she didn't like Arnie much, especially seeing he gave no apology to her mother. He definitely wasn't the same caliber as her father. She wondered why her mother had invited him. The fact that he'd never been invited before and was dancing so close also just didn't seem right. What was he doing? It didn't seem right.

Never seeing her mother dance before, Betty was surprised at the grace and timing she showed while in that man's arms, which didn't help the unfriendly feeling she was having toward him. She'd be glad when the party was over and Arnie would go home. Tomorrow she'd suggest they go to Strem's. Strem's was a lovely place. She knew Mollie wanted to get a special gift for her cousin Gracie. It's a kind of place that made Mollie happy, letting her become lost in an elegant world of fashion, attention, and friendship. She'd been a client for years and had become very fond of the owner, Miss Strem.

Angela Maria Josphina had come to America after the war to find relief from the horror and devastation done to her native Austria and to recover from the death of her fiancé, who was accidently killed in the heat of battle, when a poisonous gas canister was wildly thrown, landing on his foot. The canister broke open. Its deadly fumes killed him and another boy almost immediately; never fully recovering from the loss, Angela never married. Minneapolis offered her a new life, money, freedom, and relief from the strict Victorian rules of Europe and a fresh place to start again.

The next afternoon while Betty and Mollie sat in the living room, tea in hand, Betty asked, "Mother, why didn't you say something to Arnie about spilling champagne on you yesterday?"

"I don't know. I guess I was too surprised. I didn't want to cause a scene. Everything seemed to happen so fast."

"I think he should have said something."

"You're right. He should have," Mollie agreed, sipping the tea, today's choice a soothing chamomile.

"That's right. What kind of manners does he have?"

"You're right again," she said, taking another sip.

"Mother"—Betty paused, as if waiting to give herself permission to ask her mother—"what is your relationship with him? He's nothing to us. Daddy never invited him to play golf or go fishing. They weren't friends. Did you think they were?"

Mollie was a bit startled by the question. Her answer was slow in coming; she'd never thought about it. Betty was right; Frank had never invited Arnie to play golf, and they'd never been to each other's houses. She now wondered why. Was she sorry for him, or was it because he was a widower and had to take care of Alice? She realized the answer was no. She really didn't like him, but she was sorry for him.

"Darling, I don't have a relationship with him, but I did have fun, despite the fact he spilt champagne on me. I haven't danced like that in a long time. I'm surprised I still can."

"Maybe you haven't, but there are better choices for dance partners."

"I know. I doubt your father would have approved."

"Probably not."

"We need a trip to Strem's. It will be nice to see Angela again, to see what's new, and I do want to get something special for Gracie," Mollie suggested, changing the subject from Arnie to her cousin in Montana.

"That's right. Auntie Gracie's birthday is just around the corner." Betty remembered.

The afternoon was time well spent. Mollie bought two dresses, a skirt, and a dress for Betty and a baby-blue cardigan for Gracie Whittich Johnson. Due to the closeness in their ages and that of their children, Mollie and Gracie acted more like sisters than aunt and niece.

Sadly this wasn't true for Gracie's sons, Fred and Evert. There was no love lost between the boys even in the best or closest of times. Fred adored Uncle Frank; Evert didn't. He was jealous of the Carey money and position, showing it in various subtle but obvious ways whenever he could. Fred was so glad when Frank, Mollie, and Betty would come to the ranch to visit. He loved Uncle Frank's generosity, be it spending one-on-one time with him or taking everyone to the movies or buying ice cream, which his father never did.

One night several months later, he and Evert overheard their parents talking about the financial help they'd gotten from Frank that month. Gracie cried at the thought of Frank again stepping up, generously giving them the money for the ranch's mortgage that month and money to pay the feed bill, plus extra cash. Evert somehow knew the truth, and it made him white with resentment and anger. His thoughts raged. "How dare Frank (not even Uncle Frank) pay for anything!" His father took care of things. What kind of lie was his mother spewing? Sadly, the truth was that his father's constant disregard for business, money, and responsibility kept his family in a financial mess and him in debt to Frank, which simply increased this anger and jealousy Evert felt, distancing him further from his brother and the closeness Fred had with the Careys.

Frank never let Mollie know of this, but she did. She knew Gracie needed her love as she needed Gracie's. One afternoon, as they walked about the place, the truth came tumbling out. Mollie's heart went out to her niece. She knew none of it was Gracie's fault. She was stuck out there, in the wilds, at the mercy of a man who had no idea how to run things, doing the best she could to raise those two boys. The situation between Gracie and Don was in a constant flux, never seeming to improve. Day in and day out Gracie went forward, slowly building up a private retreat around herself, which she allowed herself to crawl into when things were really tough, and out when things were better, being careful not to let anyone, especially the boys, see it. She was the mother, the pivot, the one who makes things turn out as best she could. The sweater would be beautiful on Gracie. Mollie was glad she could give it to her and wanted to put it in the mail the next day.

When they arrived home, Mollie was in a special sentimental mood. Was it being at Strem's and seeing Angela, getting the sweater for Gracie, or thinking of what Frank would have thought of the party last night and of her dancing with Arnie that made her want to show Betty some of the old photographs from days before? Most likely she just wanted to remind herself of how wonderful Frank was and that she really didn't have any feelings for Arnie, except that he danced very well and she had fun.

She made tea and brought it into the living room, handing Betty a cup and then taking one for herself. Sitting down on the couch, sipping the tea, she looked over at Betty.

"Speaking earlier of your father, I want to show you some photographs of him, granted they are old photographs." Mollie reached for Betty's hand. She put down her cup, following her mother upstairs into the attic.

"Oh, Mother, it's so dusty and smelly up here. Where's the light I've forgotten."

"Pull down on the string at the top of the stairs." Betty did as directed. The light shined into a large room filled very systematically with neat rows and piles of boxes and other things.

"I wonder where those photographs are. Your father was such a dandy—tall, thin, clean-shaven, except for the nicest moustache. He was so good-looking. Oh, Betty, I think they're over behind that old chaise. Would you bring them here? Just put them on the table. You know this was the first piece of furniture your father and I had. It was a wedding present from Gracie's mother. It went so well with the couch Aunt Florence and Uncle Paul gave."

"Mother, there are a lot of pictures here. Do you want them all?" Betty asked, leaning over to take part of them to the table.

"Yes, please. It will be fun to see them again."

It took Betty three trips to get all the pictures on the table.

"Who are all the people?"

"Let me look. Oh, this is your father and me at our wedding. This is where he took me on our honeymoon, and this one is me when I was sixteen." Mollie said softly, almost in a dreamy way, remembering the way she felt then and how much she adored her Frank.

"You were so beautiful, and look at Daddy. My, he was really handsome. I like his moustache. Is this one of Fred and Evert?"

"Yes, yes, it is. Notice how barren the ranch looked back then. It's changed a lot since."

"It sure has. Mother, what is that painting?"

"What painting?" Mollie asked, not remembering that there were any paintings up there.

"It's charming. It's leaning against the wall, on the floor. It's of a sleeping cherub," Betty said, taking it out and then adding, "Gee, it's charming."

"It is pretty, but it doesn't fit the house," Mollie said flatly, trying not to put any importance on it.

"I see it's painted by E. Leveroos. Who is that? I like it."

Mollie flinched upon seeing the painting again. It hadn't been a part of her life since she and Frank got Betty. Clearly remembering that day when Betty came with the painting and a photograph of Helen holding her and a little note saying, "If Betty Gray wanted to know who her people were, these would tell her." The first thing Mollie did upon getting Betty settled was to put the painting and photograph in the attic. They hadn't been touched or seen since.

"I don't know, darling," Mollie lied, knowing very well that E. Leveroos was Betty's family name before it became Carey.

"Mother, look here. There's a photograph of a woman holding me. I've never seen this either. It is me, right? She's a nice-looking lady. Who is she?" Betty asked, holding up the photograph. Realizing the photo wasn't in a frame, just open, she continued asking, "Why doesn't it have a frame?"

Mollie felt her stomach tighten. What was she to say? The truth was the last thing she wanted to tell. Betty was hers, not Helen's; and she didn't want Betty looking for Helen or the Leverooses.

"That picture was taken so long ago. It's a picture of you with one of the girls who worked for us, but I don't remember her name. There was a time we had a lot of girls coming and going. It was in the middle of the war. So much happened and so many people were around. She left soon after that picture was taken I remember. I never saw her again. It's getting dark. Let's go back downstairs," Mollie suggested, hoping Betty would not be inquisitive enough to come back to take another longer look, especially at the photograph of Helen.

"All right," Betty agreed, putting the picture back against the wall, leaving the one of herself and Helen in front. They went downstairs into the kitchen.

"Betty, since it's been such a nice day, I think it would be fun for me to make your first cocktail," Mollie said, hoping for anything to distract Betty from asking about the painting and especially the photo.

"That's a lovely idea. What are you going to make?" she asked as they walked into the kitchen.

"I think we should start off your education with Pink Ladies."

"Sounds beautiful. How are they made?" Betty wanted to know.

"Four parts gin, one teaspoon grenadine, one teaspoon cream, one teaspoon lemon juice, an egg white, and, of course, ice. We put all that into Daddy's cocktail shaker then shake like mad for a few moments. Finally we strain it into cocktail glasses," Mollie explained, getting the glasses and ingredients ready.

"That doesn't seem too hard. What do you want me to do?"

"Hand me the cocktail shaker. It's in the cupboard with the liquor. Next let's put in the gin. Would you measure it?"

"Okay," Betty said, handing Mollie the shaker. Carefully she poured the gin into her father's monogrammed jigger, carefully counting off four additions, putting each into the shaker.

"Now we need to add the grenadine, the lemon juice and the cream. Would you squeeze the lemon and separate the egg? I'll get the ice. This is going to be so good. I know you'll like it," Mollie directed. When everything was put into the shaker she let Betty do the honors.

"It makes a lot of noise."

"It certainly does," Mollie said, looking forward to the result.

Slowly Betty poured the drink into the glasses.

Raising her glass, Mollie toasted her daughter, saying, "To my wonderful drink maker."

Betty smiled taking her first sip. "This is not only pretty but tastes divine."

"You've done a good job. Maybe we should enroll you in bartending school," Mollie teased.

"Oh, Mother!" She paused, taking another sip. "Is there such a thing?"

"I don't know. Maybe not." Mollie smiled also taking another sip as the doorbell rang. She got up to answer. Opening the door she recognized the very handsome young man standing there.

"Hello. I'm Kevin MacArthur. I know I've come unexpectedly, but as I was driving by, I wondered if Betty was at home. Mrs. Carey, it was such a lovely party the other night." Kevin smiled, offering his hand.

"Thank you. I'm glad you enjoyed yourself. Betty is in the living room. Won't you come in," Mollie said, eyeing the fellow. "Betty, your friend Kevin MacArthur is here."

"Really?" Betty said, putting her glass down, walking into the entryway. "Kevin. Hello. What brings you here?"

"I just happened to be driving by and wanted to thank you again for including me in the party the other night. I hope I haven't come at an inconvenient time. I'm sorry to come uninvited."

"No. Come in?"

"Thank you.".

Mollie began to wonder about the real reason he'd come. People didn't just drop in; they called first. This was strange behavior. Maybe it was some new young idea about etiquette. In any case he was here now.

"Can I take your coat and hat?" Mollie asked, handing them to Betty, who put them in the closet. Coming closer, Mollie wanted to get a better look at him. The first thing she saw was what a really handsome man he was. Betty had good taste. He was fairly tall, about five feet ten inches or so, with dark-brown hair that was combed back, letting his wonderful eyes shine at her. He looked Irish, she realized. With "MacArthur" as a surname, he probably was. She didn't like the Irish; in the old country they were poor and had terrible reputations as thieves and beggars. They also tended to be actors; she really hoped he wasn't an actor.

"I'd like to go to see the movie *Captain Blood*. Would you like to see it too?" Kevin confidently asked.

"Tell me about it."

"Well, it's about a young Irish doctor who is exiled as a slave in Barbados, where he captures a Spanish galleon. It's an action film," he explained, smiling.

"Who's in it?" she asked.

"Errol Flynn and Olivia de Havilland. I know you like them." He smiled.

"Yes. I really like her. She has such a gentle and true look about her, and I like her voice. Okay."

"Terrific! Mrs. Carey, I'll have Betty home about ten." Kevin smiled at Betty's mother she smiled back. When they get back she'd have some questions about his family and him. In the meantime, she hoped they enjoyed the movie.

Betty went to the closet to get their coats. Helping Betty with hers, Kevin smiled again at Mrs. Carey. She didn't seem to be such a bad old doll. He noticed Betty didn't look anything like her mother. Betty was tall and thin; Mrs. Carey was short and plump. Not thinking much about the difference, he was just glad to spend some time with Betty and to see this new movie.

By the time they got to the theater, the lobby was jammed. People, waiting to buy their tickets and get a good seat, milled around. Slowly the line shortened, and they inched their way closer to the ticket booth. Kevin bought two tickets, and they continued through the lobby to the doors of the theater, where a nice-looking young usher took the tickets from Kevin and directed them to the center door. It wasn't dark yet, and conversation from the crowd was loudly muted. Kevin spotted two seats together about eight rows from the screen; everything else had been taken. He led her down the aisle and told her to hold the seat beside hers for him; he'd be back. Betty sort of climbed over several couples and then took off her coat as she sat down in the second seat. She put her coat across her lap and tucked her purse beside the seat designated for Kevin. He got back just as the lights were going down. Sitting down, he handed her a box of popcorn. The curtain was drawn and the magic of movies began: the newsreel, a really good Mickey Mouse cartoon, and finally the feature—*Captain Blood* starring Errol Flynn and Olivia de Havilland, whose names blazed onto the screen. Everyone was quiet.

Kevin quietly opened the box of popcorn, offering it to Betty. She took some, slowly eating it as the story began. When they'd finished the popcorn, Kevin took her hand. She gently wrapped her fingers around his palm, enjoying the sweetness of holding hands in the dark. When there were tense moments in Captain Blood's life, she tightly gripped his hand, releasing it when the excitement was over. This movie intrigued both of them—such adventure, such passion between Errol and Olivia, and such an ending.

"Oh, Kevin, I loved it! It was so much fun," Betty said, releasing his hand.

"I did too. Let's go for a little walk."

"I'd like that."

Leaving the theater, they turned left, just slowly walking toward Kevin's parked car. He took her hand again, gently swinging it as they looked at the store windows. Betty wanted to keep the memory of his hand, the actor's hand, folded around her fingers. She liked Kevin more than she should have. Who could resist that handsome face and that voice? She loved when she could watch him in rehearsal. His voice, strong and believable, made each part his own. It all seemed so easy as she watched him in *Macbeth* or in a Sheridan farce or an impromptu sketch. Betty wasn't sure what feelings lay inside her toward Kevin, but whatever they were, they were strong, the best part being, she felt, that they would be good friends forever. There was no push of reality saying Kevin was taboo, but she, deep down, knew her mother was very anti-Irish. She wouldn't give him up so easily—mother's fears or not.

"What do you think of the fashion this year?" he asked.

"I don't know. It's similar to last year, which was similar to the year before that," she answered, adding, "But I like the shoes now."

"The shoes?" he asked.

"Yes. They're prettier now and seem more feminine."

"Look at the old lady walking toward us. Are her shoes pretty? I think they make her look like she's just come off the farm." Kevin looked down, watching her matronly shoes slowly almost shuffle toward them.

"Maybe she has. I agree they aren't very nice, but maybe they're comfortable, if she has to walk for a long way," Betty suggested.

"The designers have to make them pretty and practical," he suggested flatly.

"I agree, but style has always been the important thing, and the way it's going now I think style will win out over anything too practical," Betty said, watching the old lady come up to them and then pass by. There was nothing interesting about her—her colors drab, her shoes even drabber, and she looked colorless, almost unloved. Maybe she was a widow. In any case the old lady was no concern of either of them, so they let her slip quietly by without a further thought.

Upon reaching the car, Kevin unlocked the passenger's door, letting Betty get in. As she did, he noticed what beautiful legs she had—fairly thin but very well-shaped. She had expensive silk stockings of a lovely beige shade. He wondered if her being a horsewoman was why she was so well-proportioned and sexy. There was a wonderful sexiness about her he realized she was totally unaware of. It was what made her so intriguing, not to mention her wonderful mind. It was actually her mind that caught his attention. She was quick in thought and speech, but she was gentle, loving, and generous in heart; and he just plain liked her. He'd been intrigued by the difference between like and love and had come to the conclusion that like was more important; like was the glue that kept love coming. He didn't know when he'd discovered this, but he fully realized its truth. He really liked Betty; she was so easy to be with, and she was fun.

Betty also felt that special something toward Kevin, handsome Kevin, whose big expressive eyes kept her thinking of what he was thinking, but mostly she liked him because he was interesting. She didn't know guys like him, thoughtful, sincere, and genuine, and he didn't try to take advantage of her. She knew with a name like MacArthur he was most likely Catholic, but who cared? Maybe her mother did, but she didn't. He was kind and smart, and when he took her hand, he made her happy. The simple pleasures of life, often small and unnoticeable sometimes, made the biggest statement, saying volumes with little effort. Hand holding was in this class, and she liked, really liked, Kevin.

It didn't take long to get to Lake of the Isles Boulevard. The Carey house was the only one that had the porch light on, waiting for Betty's return. Mollie was already upstairs and undressed. She sat in an overstuffed bedroom chair reading *Alice Adams* by Booth Tarkington. She'd seen the new movie reviews of it and was looking forward to seeing just how Katharine Hepburn would portray the inquisitive Alice. She hoped she and Betty could go to see it on Saturday. Mollie liked Katharine Hepburn. She was so beautiful to watch—the way she moved, almost in a sweeping staccato motion, sure and proud, knowing. Mollie wondered if she was like that in real life, and further thoughts about her and her affair with Spencer Tracy made her think so. It was Hollywood—they were often out of control, at least according to what the movie magazines reported. She heard Betty's key turn in the locked door, opening it. She called up to her mother, announcing their return.

"Mother, I've brought Kevin back. I'm going to make him a cup of coffee. Would you like one too?"

"No, thank you, darling. Please tell Mr. MacArthur good night for me," Mollie called back, putting a bookmark in page 30 and then laying the book on the little table beside the chair. She stood up and headed for her room.

"Okay, Mother," Betty answered, turning to take Kevin to the kitchen. "My mother wishes you a good night."

"Thank you. My, this is a big kitchen," he said, looking around at all the storage there was in the room. "My mother has a nice kitchen too, but not like this."

"We often entertain. We've got a lot of dishes, silverware, and linens because of it, not to mention all the cooking pots and pans needed to cook for large parties."

"Why do you entertain so much?" he asked, looking around the room again.

"My father had a large grain company. Can you believe Woodrow Wilson and his wife were guests several times? So was Herbert Hoover and his wife. We even have a special set of china Mother calls the Hoover china. Being responsible for feeding Europe after World War I was a very personal project of Daddy's. It was this work that brought the friendships with Wilson, Hoover, and their wives. I loved it when these people came. They were all so interesting to listen to, and I used to get to stay up late to be with them," Betty told him. He smiled as though he didn't quite believe her but changed his mind when later he saw photographs of them in the Careys' library.

"Really?"

"Yes. Would you like some coffee?"

"That would be nice. Herbert Hoover, my!"

"The Hoovers have been friends since Daddy was in the Chicago Board of Trade."

"Really," he repeated.

"Yes, when I was just a little girl. We lived in Chicago for one year while he was its president," she said as she made coffee for them.

Coffee making was a mundane job, but Betty liked cooking—not that she got to do much. Mostly she watched as their cook Alice did all the measuring, stirring, and cutting, always creating something good. Betty wanted, one day, to be a great cook, to entertain her friends and husband as her parents had done.

"I'm impressed you know such famous people. The only important person I can think of I know is Santa Claus, but I really don't know him."

Betty began to laugh at that. Kevin was so funny at times. He just seemed to lighten her spirits without trying.

"Santa Claus is in a very special class. I bet President Wilson and Herbert Hoover would also like to know him. Maybe they do." She chuckled as Kevin began to laugh.

"I bet. Can you imagine what they would ask for?" he teased.

"I doubt it would be for a new sled," she said, still kind of laughing. "To change the subject, would you help me run lines for my theater exam?"

"Sure, I'd be glad to. What do you want me to do?"

"I need you to read the next line in the script that has been given to me for the exam. Everyone got something different," he told her. "I was given a scene written by our teacher. It's about a young man who is sick. He's being helped at home by a strict nurse. He feels he won't get well, even though the nurse does everything she can to convince him he will."

"It sounds heavy," Betty said, hoping she'd be able to do what he wanted.

"I guess it is. I think I've got the emotion down, but I still need someone to run lines, to play off," he said, feeling Betty could portray the emotion from the nurse. He really just needed to hear the dialogue, to catch the reminder words for his next line.

"When would you like to do it?" she asked, pouring the coffee into two cups.

"How about tomorrow?"

"That would be fine. Where?"

"Could we do it here after class?" he asked, adding a little sugar to his cup.

"I can't imagine why not." Betty smiled, thinking it would be fun.

She was sorry she never took an acting class. Somehow it almost seemed the natural thing to do. If things went well with helping Kevin, maybe she'd seriously think about taking an acting class next semester.

Slowly they drank the coffee as Kevin explained a little about the scene. "I sure do appreciate all of this, but I'm especially glad of your friendship," he said, looking at her in a soft, almost loving, way.

She liked the way he was looking at her and smiled. She always felt they had something more than just friendship between them.

"I'll be here at four," he said, finishing up his coffee.

"Okay. Would you like a little more coffee?"

"I better not. I've got to run, big day tomorrow. You really make good coffee."

"Thank you. I learned from a very good teacher."

They walked to the big, heavy front door. Betty got his coat and hat for him. As he put them on, she opened the door. Turning toward the open door to go out, he quickly turned back and gently kissed her cheek in a brotherly way. He then kissed her again; this time he gave a sweet, gentle kiss, but on the lips. Holding her for a moment, he thanked her for the evening and her help in running his lines. She felt glowing as she watched him go down the walk to his car. Slowly she closed and locked the door. Turning out the lights, she then put the cups on the kitchen table and headed upstairs.

"Betty, did Mr. MacArthur leave?" Mollie asked.

"Yes, just now," she answered, coming into Mollie's room and sitting down beside her on the bed.

"Did you have a nice time?" Mollie asked, putting her hand up to touch Betty's hair, stroking it back.

"Yes. He is so nice, Mother. He kissed me tonight at the door as he left," Betty confessed, smiling.

"My! Did you kiss him back?" Mollie wanted to know. She'd never found time to talk to Betty about becoming involved too quickly, of not believing the first one was the only one. She was beginning to feel sorry now but realized that Betty was a smart girl and, she hoped, wouldn't jump directly into the fire, not thinking at all that this is what happened to her when she met Frank. Then this thought surfaced.

"I did. He was so sweet. Oh, Mother, I really like him," Betty confessed in an unexpected tone of voice, surprising Mollie, who gasped a little while trying to keep it in. She knew it would come; Betty was at the right age, and he was very good-looking. Nature was nature, but he was Irish and Betty was not.

"Well, that's very nice," Mollie said, beginning to worry about the possible coming storm about him.

Betty went on to tell her, "He asked me to help him for his drama exam. He asked me to run lines with him."

"Run lines? Isn't that something football players do?" Mollie asked, knowing nothing of the theater world.

"No. Running lines is when you help an actor learn his or her part by reading the other part to him. He then recites his lines," Betty explained.

"Oh, that's very interesting," Mollie said, listening to her daughter. "Kevin asked if we could do it here tomorrow after class."

"Why not? That would be fine," Mollie answered, not wanting to encourage things but wanting to find out more about him, adding, "Would Mr. MacArthur like to stay for dinner?"

"I'll ask him." Betty smiled, adding, "I really like him."

"I'm glad, darling. I liked your father right away too."

Betty smiled. Her father was the best. She really didn't think any man could measure up to him, but Kevin was so nice, good-looking and dreamy.

"Mother, could we have lamb chops and hash brown potatoes for tomorrow's dinner?"

"That's a good idea. Does Mr. MacArthur like lamb?"

"I don't know. I hope so. I love it."

"Me too. I'll tell cook tomorrow when she comes in. We should have a nice green salad, and how about apple pie with cheddar cheese for dessert?"

"Perfect. I'm sure he'll love it."

He isn't much of an Irishman if he doesn't, Mollie thought but said, "Good, we'll plan on it."

"Mother, you are so wonderful. Thank you."

"It's the least I can do, Betty dear."

"I think I'll go work on the Chaucer homework I have."

Betty already had a fair idea of what the professor wanted. He'd given several choices: to write a ten-page essay on his early writings, middle writings, or his last writings.

"Alright, darling. I'll see you later."

At that, Mollie went into the living room, sat down in Frank's chair, and opened the book she was reading to revisit the young family in Wyoming, struggling with establishing their homestead.

As she began to read, she found herself drifting off with thoughts of Frank buzzing around her. She began to wonder if Betty could possibly like Mr. MacArthur as much as she did Frank when they first met. Thoughts, dreamy thoughts, of their first kiss came—how his hand touched her back and face, then went down her leg. How she gently protested but didn't. Then how his kisses became increasingly passionate. She began to sigh a little. What she wouldn't give to kiss her dear Frank just one more time. She felt so desirous of his love and attention. To be so close and kissed by him was all she could think of. He was everything—good-looking, kind, soft-spoken, and very amusing. He simply took her breath away. All of a sudden she woke with a start. It was Betty coming down to say good night. "Did I scare you, Mother? I'm sorry," Betty said, touching Mollie's shoulder.

"Yes, a little, I must admit. I was having such a nice dream about your father," she said, smiling.

Betty was a little surprised. She never thought about Mollie dreaming about her father. She never really thought that older people had thoughts or dreams of the ones they loved.

"What were you dreaming?"

"Believe it or not, it was about our first kiss. I don't know if I should be telling you such things." Mollie smiled that same remembering smile.

"Yes, you should. I'd like to know."

Betty looked at Mollie, who began to laugh.

"I bet you never thought about us in that way. Well, I can tell you there was a lot of that before you came along," Mollie confessed shyly, putting her head down, surprised at herself for what she'd just said. "I think it's beautiful."

"It was, and I'm still in love with your father. He was just the best and the only one for me."

"I hope I feel that way someday."

"I hope so too. You know, dear, we must stay within our own rank, within our own area of society. Sadly society dictates so many things about the people we deal with, and in order to be involved with society, we have to follow the rules."

Betty looked at her mother. Had she broken some rules? What was being said?

"I don't know what you mean? What society? What rules?" she asked. "Usually people of our means don't associate with others outside."

"What do you mean?" Betty asked.

"Usually people of various groups tend to stay together."

"You mean like whites or blacks or Asians or Indians staying together?"

"That's right. It also goes for religions and people adhering to their religions. Usually people don't marry outside their own faith."

"That's all very interesting, but what does that have to do with me?" Betty asked.

"Nothing for the moment. I just want you to remember where you belong."

Betty was dumbfounded by this conversation. This was a new, different side of her mother showing itself. Never a word of race or religion was spoken either for one or against another. Now this conversation. It all seemed so strange. Betty let it drop. She wasn't going to concern herself with it.

Chapter 12

The same evening Betty went with Kevin MacArthur to see *Captain Blood*. Helen arrived in Vienna. She had a letter of introduction from Max Schmidt, the man responsible for so many movie successes in Hollywood. Max was a tyrant at the studio, but a pushover in real life. If he liked you, he'd move heaven and earth for you to make you into something, which he did for Helen. He liked her style of acting, her sense of each part they'd worked on together, and her loyalty to the profession. He liked her but was powerless to the changing times and demands the public made for more blondes, more sex and youth, and more reality. He knew Helen's thirty-plus years put her at the end of her movie career in America. Europe, Germany, and Austria, that's where he felt she should be.

Max had a friend in Munich, the renowned director Adolph Rubin, who was looking for women of Helen's talent. He wanted Americans, people he felt would bring a fresh face to the screen. When Max introduced them, he was so impressed he immediately cast her as Elizabeth, Empress of Austria, in a historical drama about her assassination. The film was to be shot in Vienna. Three weeks later, Helen was there, but before she put her foot on Austrian soil, Max arranged for the noted teacher Fritz Braun to give her German lessons, which began in earnest, immediately. He carefully but intensely taught her the basics, enough so she could converse on an easy level. He also taught her some history of the area, plus insight into the food, giving her a sense of the beauty and culture of the country. Through the lessons she had become intrigued by Europe. Everything pulled her up into a cloud of fascinating newness. Everything was so wonderfully different, bringing new adventures and fun every day. All of this began to pay off.

The first day's shoot was spent with Adolph working on lighting, making sure the set was exactly what he wanted and that the actors were ready. Helen was. She quickly learned what he wanted. He was a tough master, like Max. They would have nothing less than perfection from everyone. Adolph's growing reputation was on the line. As the morning progressed, Adolph decided the empress's dress wasn't right. The seamstress led Helen back to the dressing area and almost tore the dress off her. There was a flurry of fabric and sewing, all redone within an hour. Adolph was satisfied and the shoot continued.

It was a gray day. A little rain fell, and then the sun came out for a bit, and then it clouded up again, putting the director in a furious mood. Helen didn't know films were shot in bits and pieces, not from beginning to end as was done in the theater. So much of it had to do with lighting. When the shoot was done inside the studio, outside noise was the enemy. Today's scene was of the empress riding from her castle to town, getting out of the carriage with her lady-in-waiting and her private secretary, going into a millinery shop, and ordering one hundred hats.

Helen learned that this was Elizabeth's strange regular habit. She ordered everything by the hundred. After she was back in the carriage, her secretary would go back to cancel ninety-nine of whatever was ordered. It was later revealed that this ordering everything in one hundred lots was one of the odd quirks associated with her growing madness. Helen was glad she had read of the empress and knew a little of her and her problems. It helped her imagine how the empress could think nothing of ordering one hundred of anything.

Adolph was finally satisfied after twenty takes, telling everyone of a job well done at about 9:00 p.m.

At six the next morning, Helen sat getting her makeup done and then her costume on. Again it was a gray day, and Adolph was in a foul mood. As the day progressed, the sun came out, improving his mood, making everyone on the set less nervous. He was happy and honored to tell everyone things were going forward, plus there was a guest coming to the set. Count Heinrich Harrisch had asked to see what the movie studio was all about and wanted to see how Elizabeth was being portrayed. He'd been intrigued by this art form and was fascinated by it.

Count Harrisch arrived quietly, not wanting to interrupt the filming. He parked his silver Austro-Daimler convertible along the road, got out, and walked the short distance to the shoot site. Just as expected, for a post WWI gentleman, the count's casual brown trench coat smelled slightly of gasoline, and there were a few oil spots on his sleeve. The coat was worn over an elegant, light-brown tweed suit with a dark-brown velvet collar; a brown silk ascot; dark-brown, high-topped laced boots and light-brown deerskin driving gloves, which he removed and put inside the pocket of the coat. He wore a dark-brown fedora. Arriving at the set, he found things to be in a strange order, cameras all over, huge lights everywhere, some disassembled, some not, a lot of people milling about and a lot of noise. There were people talking and yelling for someone to pull this, move that, and get something else.

Just as Adolf called for the camera to be put on several big boxes so the scene could be filmed from another angle, he happened to get a glimpse of the count walking toward him. Recognizing the man, he introduced himself.

"Good morning, Count Harrisch." He bowed slightly.

"Good morning."

"I'm Adolf Rubin, the director of the film. Welcome to the set." He extended his hand.

The count took it, giving a strong handshake. "Thank you. You have a very busy place here."

"That"—he paused, looking at the count's elegant clothing—"it is."

"I think it is very interesting the movie is being made about Empress Elizabeth. I remember her quite fondly. She was one of the most beautiful women in Austria," he said, smiling at his remembrance of her.

"After having seen her portrait, I would agree. I'd like to escort you around, if I may."

"Please do. It all looks so interesting."

"It is. Please be careful where you step. There are lots of pieces of equipment in use."

"What's it all for?" he asked, stepping over a box.

"Basically it's used to create the right feeling for the film. With the lights we can convey day or night, inside or outside effects. Through the set, place and sometimes time can be shown. We do many other things to make it all seem real, believable, and interesting. It's important to make the audience believe what they are seeing and to feel the story."

"I see," the count said, starting to find the whole thing makes sense. "In about ten minutes we are going to shoot a scene over here, between Empress Elizabeth and her son. Come," Adolf said, getting a chair for the count, putting it to the left of his own but clearly out of the way.

While Helen got into place, the tallish, well-grayed, distinguished, intelligent, fifty-plus-year-old count saw her. His relatively thin lips parted into a smile, exposing his clean, white teeth. His intense blue eyes twinkled. The official look on his face turned into a friendly openness. He liked her. She was young and fresh, something new for him.

The count had never married, always saying he wouldn't marry just anyone. He dedicated his life to Austria, making her his love, but this woman caught his eye.

"Adolf, introduce me to the lady over there in the light-blue dress," he said.

"My pleasure, but when we finish the scene," he whispered to him, calling out loudly, "Quiet on the set! Places! Action!"

At that, the scene began. Helen came out into the middle of the room, sat down on an elaborate needlepoint couch, looked straight into the camera, and called to her lady-in-waiting to prepare things for them to go to Switzerland. Another spur-of-the-moment trip.

About two minutes into the scene, Adolf yelled out, "Cut. Heinz, go outside and block off the street. I can hear a car. Helen, when you say 'I want the pink dresses, both of them,' say it with more intensity, and don't look at the lady-in-waiting. Look toward the door—you're expecting your son."

Helen smiled and then nodded, letting him know she understood.

Adolf again called out "action," and again Helen entered the room. A moment later one of the big lights fell, causing a huge crash. Again "cut" was called and everyone went to the side to wait for it to be uprighted. A third time the scent began. This time it went smoothly.

Adolf was pleased at this last attempt and called out for everyone to get ready for the next scene, and then lunch. The count sat quietly, just watching the flurry of excitement, thinking movies are like the parliament, a lot of nothing and then some action. He smiled.

After the lunch break, a moment after Adolf called for action, part of the set fell.

"What next," he mumbled. "Crew, put the set back up, and be careful about it and quick. Time is money," he growled, literally like a lion.

At that moment, without any formal introduction or protocol, the count decided to speak to Helen. Walking toward her, his heart raced a little.

"Good day. I'm Count Heinrich Harrisch. This moviemaking is such an interesting thing." He offered his hand.

Helen looked straight into his serious face, seeing a slight family resemblance. Something about the eyes, and of course, his manner was such—royal and confident but approachable. His voice was quiet, gentle, and clear. It was a voice that caught one's attention, trustworthy.

Taking his hand, she felt a sense of assurance. This man knew what he wanted.

"Good day. I'm Helen Leveroos. You must be our guest. I'm so glad you could come visit the set." She smiled at him.

"I've become very interested in what you do. I mean how movies are made," he said, just looking at her. She seemed so gentle, so ladylike, so kind, and so womanly. He noticed her eyes seemed to examine him, enticing him to her level.

"Movies are very interesting to make, but they take lots of time," she explained, feeling the strength of his gaze. Not even Goff had looked at her like that. *Were all European men so intense?* she wondered.

"They are also very noisy to make. Do things like that fall often?" he asked.

"No, sometimes, but not usually." She smiled at the charmingly naive question.

"Today must be an exception," he said.

"I think so. Adolf has been in a special mood, trying to get everything right. Sometimes he's a demon, and sometimes he's a pussycat."

The count lightly laughed at Helen's choice of words. She seemed so easy with him, no fear of formal protocol, so American.

"Where are you staying? Would it be possible for you to have dinner with me this evening?" he asked, his heart beating a little faster, fearing an answer of no.

"I don't know why not. I don't know anybody here other than the crew, and I'm constantly with them. It would be lovely, but I do have to be back at the hotel early. I have to be on the set at six in the morning for hair and wardrobe."

"I'll make sure of it. Where shall I call for you?"

"I'll be at the Grand Hotel," she answered, looking into his lonely eyes. "I'll see you at six." He smiled, picked up her hand, brought it to his lips, and lightly kissed it.

"I'm looking forward to it." She smiled. She'd never had her hand kissed before and was impressed by the honor. "Please excuse me. I'm needed back on the set. Why don't you stay and watch for a while, if you have time."

"All right . . . I also have things to do," he said, gesturing her back into the empress's life.

Chapter 13

Helen was finished by five and was back at the hotel by five thirty.

Her mind raced. "What should I wear? This man knows quality. Oh dear."

Looking through the choices in the closet, she finally decided on a dark-green top and matching skirt. It gave her a look of importance, nicely setting off her dark blonde hair. She chose simple pearls for her neck and pearl earrings to match. She was set. As she dressed, she thought about the count.

Count Heinrich is a real count. He really knew Empress Elizabeth. Should I talk to him about the empress or about America, Minneapolis, and St. Paul? Should I tell him of my life or ask about his? Should I mention Betty Gray? Maybe I should let him do all the talking. Yes, that's the answer. It doesn't bother me he seems to be older. I wonder how old he is . . . not important. I'm not going to marry him.

As the count dressed, he also thought about the upcoming evening. *She was so beautiful.* His thoughts then began to turn to the obvious difference in age between them. *Would she be seriously interested in someone older?* He didn't want her to think of him in a fatherly way. He didn't want to be her father.

Standing in front of the full-length mirror in his dressing room, he brushed his silvery gray hair into place. He was satisfied with his appearance; navy blue pants, freshly ironed white linen shirt, light-gray silk ascot, and matching navy blue jacket, with special silver buttons embossed with his coat of arms. His black boots were polished to the ultimate shine. Turning toward the table in the center of the room, he picked up his official photograph he wanted to give to her. He carefully put it into a navy blue leather frame, inside a special presentation box bearing his coat of arms. He put it in his coat pocket.

His steps were light as he left his bedroom, the walls of which were decorated with gold leaves and matching cupboards. He did stop for a moment to close the window. Entering the wide hallway, he made his way down the stairs and to the entrance hall with its light-blue walls painted with striking ferns and exotic flowers. He called for his car to be brought to the front.

As the car was delivered he put on his brown trench coat and matching brown deerskin gloves, which both lightly smelled of gasoline. Getting into his silver Austro-Daimler convertible, he smiled. He loved this car. Very soon he'd be with the gametglecth Helen. Fifteen minutes later Helen sat beside him in the car. She had never seen such a car. It was beautiful and what a machine, purring all the while taking them to a charming, small restaurant about three kilometers into the countryside.

The restaurant was just a small inn, but the count had loved it since his teens. He'd often gone there to get away from the flurry of royal duty. The fresh air and gentle breeze, mixed with singing birds and greenness, somehow brought him strength to continue with his job. They made a wonderful wiener-breaded fried chicken there, and he was in the mood for a good thick piece of apple strudel or a plate of walnut slices and fruit torts and lovely Rhine wine with a strong coffee to end things.

"Fraulein Helen, this is my favorite restaurant. I hope you'll like it too," he said, opening the door of his Austro-Daimler and helping her out. "I'm sure I will. I'm hungry." She smiled at him, thinking how distinguished he looked.

When they got in, the owner, Herr Schmidt, escorted them to a small table. Looking around, Helen liked the rustic look of the place. She could understand the count liked the change of pace from the palace. She realized it was a place of freedom for him—relaxing, less formal, but with everything a member of the royal family could want.

"We haven't seen you in a while, Count Heinrich. Welcome."

"Royal duties have kept me away. I'm glad to be back. Do we have the special wiener chicken tonight, and is there some apple strudel?"

"We have both. Would you like an aperitif before?" Herr Schmidt asked, smiling.

"Yes," he said, not thinking if Helen wanted a drink or not. He simply ordered a Slivovitz for himself and a glass of Mosel for her.

She smiled to herself when it arrived, thinking what a pretty glass it was brought in. A very wide clear glass bowl let the light of the room shine on the wine. The bowl was supported by a thick dark-green glass stem.

"Thank you." She looked up at the waiter and then over to Count Heinrich, nodding to him.

"Prost," he answered, clicking the little glass his Slivovitz came in with hers. "Ah, this is very fine. How is yours?"

"Very nice, sir. Thank you." She thought the place sort of reminded her of a place Goff used to take her to in Minneapolis, but without all of this ambiance.

"Fraulein Helen, please don't call me sir. We can't be friends if you call me sir. It sets up a barrier, and I don't want a distance between us. It's all right when we're in public, but not when we're alone."

"All right. What would you like me to call you?"

"My name is Heinrich."

"Heinrich. It is such a distinguished name. I'd be happy to call you Heinrich," she said, feeling somewhat strange at hearing what he said about not wanting any barriers between them. Did this mean he wanted something permanent between them, or was it royal style? She didn't know if she wanted to be in a place that might put her in something she didn't know anything about. But Heinrich was so charming, distinguished, and really handsome. Strangely enough, she felt at ease with him and very happy to be in his company. She didn't care that he was twenty years her senior or that she didn't realize his intentions.

"If I'm to call you Heinrich, you must call me Helen," she added.

"Helen, tell me about your life." His accent seemed to soften, or maybe she was beginning to get used to it.

"As you know, I work in films and on the stage," she started.

"Yes, yes, I know about that. I want to know about your life in America. What's it like there? Everything must be so free. Here we've been living under strict established rules and laws for hundreds of years. How does everything work when it's so free there?"

"I don't know. I never thought about it. I suppose it's similar to anyplace—laws tell people how to live, and most live accordingly," Helen said now, thinking about it.

"Do the laws of Boston and New York really work in the American West? I've heard that the laws are made up as the situation needs, particularly in the West."

"That's the way it used to be under people like Wyatt Earp and Doc Holiday, but that was a long time ago, even though Wyatt Earp is still living, granted he's a very old man now. I've heard he lives in Los Angeles and is pretty much a loner."

"Loner? What is a loner?" he asked, interested in the new word.

"To be a loner is someone who prefers to be alone and lives by himself, apart from others," Helen explained.

"Are there many people in America like that?"

"I don't know. America is a big place. It is easy to be alone there if you want to be."

"It is hard for me to imagine," he said, thinking about the possibility.

"Me too." She smiled.

"Excuse me, sir, the menu," the waiter interrupted.

"Thank you." He paused. "Helen, would you like me to translate."

"That would be wonderful. I can't read German yet. I'm still learning to speak it. I've got a good teacher, but I'm afraid it will take a while."

"I understand. It's a difficult language," he said, adding "They have wiener chicken and apple strudel, which I'm going to order. They also have . . ."

"That's sounds lovely. I want the same," she said, interrupting him and looking at the waiter.

"Thank you." The waiter smiled at them. "Right away. Would you care for another Slivovitz, sir?"

"Yes. Please bring another glass of wine for the lady when the food comes. Actually, bring a bottle of Mosel."

"Yes, sir."

"In America a gentleman usually asks a lady if she'd like another glass of wine," Helen said, feeling kind of kept.

"I just assumed you'd like another, since your glass is nearly empty."

"It is, isn't it? Yes, I would enjoy another with dinner," she said, looking over at him. His eyes slightly twinkled in the room's lighting. His gray hair looked like muted silver. Finally he seemed to relax a little. She hoped she hadn't spoken out of turn by telling him about men in America asking a lady questions.

"Tell me what you think of President Wilson," he began.

"Oh, I don't know. He's a tough fellow and the League of Nations is a good thing. I try not to get into such things. Politics is not for me," she answered.

"I understand your thinking. Politics can, often as not, bring about things between people which shouldn't be. I do think he's a gutsy fellow with a lot on his plate."

"I agree. I wouldn't want to be in his shoes. Far too much responsibility for me. Being in government, I know you have to be involved in the constant business of the nation."

"That's true, but I don't have to do it all alone. I've got a lot of good, solid help who strongly support the country and me."

"As it should be." She smiled proudly at him, realizing without saying a lot he'd said volumes.

"Tell me about your life in America."

"My life in America, in Minnesota, is full. The theater, my family, and friends all keep me busy."

"How long have you been in theater?"

"Since I was a child. My mother was also an actress. She did a lot of local theater. She even died on stage one night."

"Oh my! What happened?"

"She had a massive stroke. She just fell to the floor in the middle of her lines one night."

"I'm sorry. How long ago was that?"

"About two years ago. Her funeral was wonderful. So many people came to pay their respects. It was just the attention she would have loved."

He sort of laughed at that statement, saying, "I'm glad she didn't suffer."

"No, they said she didn't. We were close. She was a wonderful mother. She gave me everything I needed or could want—home, security, and love."

"You were lucky. My parents worked too but often had little time for me. Like all public people, there was always something to be done for the nation. I think they spent more time visiting orphans and orphanages than they did with me. I'm beginning to sound very jealous, but I did understand it was their job. I have to do the same, everything from visiting old-age homes to opening up new art galleries and supporting opening nights at the opera, plus all the meetings needed to run the country. It's not an easy job. I really enjoy the Spring Annual Fair. It's very interesting and, I must, say fun. I had a military career because it was expected of me. After the war I could barely recognize the changes everywhere. Life had changed as did the people."

"Your life sounds so different from mine."

"It is that, but it's tiring and lonesome. I have no one to come home to, except the servants who look after me. Even though they're devoted to me, they're not close. I've come to think they're more devoted to my family name and the house than they are to me personally."

"That's very sad. Don't you have any friends?"

"Very few."

"Well, you've got me now." She smiled at him, all of a sudden regretting what she'd just said.

"That's wonderful. I accept your friendship," he said, looking at her and thinking, *My, she's a pretty woman.*

Helen wasn't a citizen of the country, but she began to feel safe, almost as if she could be. She'd never even been in close range of any of the presidents of America and couldn't imagine what it would be like to look at, or even speak to, Mr. Wilson; but here was the count, opening his life to her, like a friend. Looking at him she sensed he needed something basic, something real. Here was this man, this royal man, projecting things she'd never experienced before from any man. She wondered if she imagined these feelings or if it were real? She wondered how he could be alone. A man of the world, alone. It didn't make sense. Was it his work that didn't let him become friends with those around him, or was he too distant? He didn't appear distant, quite the contrary.

"Helen, do you like animals? What's your favorite flower?" he asked.

"I like lots of animals. As for flowers, I love roses and lilacs. We had the most beautiful lilac bush, a huge thing, in the side yard of my childhood home. I remember I used to take my dolls outside, set them up beside that lilac, and pretend all kinds of wonderful stories with them. I remember one day our dog, Bucky, came over to see what I was doing. All of a sudden he grabbed one of my dolls and ran off with her. He took her under the neighbor's front steps and seriously chewed on her arms. When my father got her out, I cried. My poor doll had been so badly hurt. I was mad at that dog for a long time. I then began to play doctor and hospital with her. I spent long hours making her comfortable in bed, rearranging her pillows and sheets, plus making all sorts of medicines for her."

"What a wonderful story," the count said, sipping the strong drink in front of him. "I remember loving to pretend to ride a fiery horse and doing battle with the Turks, smashing and clashing and bashing them. Naturally I always won, and the Turks all went running back to Istanbul." He laughed at the remembrance of the memory. "I also remember having a wonderful big train. I could actually sit on the engine and could make it go up, down, and around its big tracks. Naturally I was always bringing supplies to the troops. Also great fun, I always felt so important." He smiled.

"Your game sounds almost more fun than mine." She smiled, taking a sip of her wine as she looked at him. She could see she was able to change the business of his mind, letting him come into her mind-set.

At that, dinner arrived. The count was hungry. He could hardly wait to see what his guest thought of the meal he'd ordered for them. He carefully poured another glass of wine from the bottle of Mosel. Again the lovely color of the freshly poured wine in her glass caught her eye.

A plate was placed in front of each of them; the aroma sparked their appetites.

The count watched as Helen carefully cut a piece of meat and put it in her mouth. He noticed she gave an *umm* sound as she chewed it. He smiled; she liked his choice.

"This is wonderful. I love the salad. It looks so lovely," Helen said, putting some lettuce and a little tomato on her fork.

"They do a good job with everything. Wait until they bring dessert, the best apple strudel in the world," he said, starting to cut another piece of the meat.

They ate slowly, enjoying the food and fine wine but mostly each other's company. She told him about Hollywood, Minneapolis, Chicago, and New York; and he told her about Austria. They ate and drank, eagerly listening to each other. It was nearly midnight when the bill was paid and he got her settled in the car.

"Helen, I know it's very late, but do you mind if I drive around the countryside? It looks so different at night, and with the full moon we have now, you'll get a very new look at things. This type of moon doesn't happen very often."

"That would be fine. I know I'm in good hands." She looked over and smiled at him. His profile looked a little sharp in the moon's lighting. It made his hair shine gently, giving it a silvery pewter color. His features appeared sharp. One could see a fineness to his mouth and a determination on his forehead and chin. He looked every bit a count, but it was more than that Helen saw. She saw a man whom she was beginning to be very fond of. She could trust him; he was solid, strong, and there. She reached over and took his hand, clinching her fingers around his hand of power, not sorry in the least for that maybe out-of-place gesture. He, in return, put his fingers through hers. Her hand seemed small and delicate, yet she held on with a tight grip. He raised her hand to his lips and gently kissed her gloved fingers. She smiled.

"I want to show you Vienna from the hills. It is very nice to see the city from another prospective." He kissed her hand again and then gently released it.

Slowly he started his beautiful Daimler, driving them through the pavements of Vienna and gradually leading them up into the hills and vineyards beyond the city. Soon, he wanted to take her to visit some of the quaint little churches in the area. Also on the list was to show her the vineyards and later to sample some of the new wine in September and, for fun, to take her for a ride on the big Ferris wheel in Prater. He wanted her life to intertwine with his in every way, every day. It was at that moment he thought of marrying her, but first he wanted her to get used to him and his lifestyle and the duties it brought. He also wanted to know more about her, to know how she might react to certain situations brought on by politics or being involved with royals. He needed to know how she would handle a possible dangerous situation, like a possible assassination attempt or a revolution—not that it would happen, God forbid. Could she handle important guests with grace and a calm demeanor? He also had to know if there was anything in her past that would cause an embarrassment to him or the state. He was sorry her past had to be delved into, but even though he loved his cousin Empress Elizabeth, he didn't want them to deal with any kind of possible problems such as Elizabeth had; the state couldn't afford it. He needed a wife who appealed to the public, not because of her looks but because of how she lived and what she did for the people. It was an important decision that had to be made with care and consideration. He knew he'd never be emperor, but he didn't want to wear a crown.

"Heinrich, this is all so beautiful. Look at the way the moonlight makes the hills and fields almost glow. It's better than any movie could bring to the imagination of an involved viewing audience."

"I'm glad you like it here. I would think you must have such views at home," he said, nervous about beginning to probe into her past. It had to be done gently and in a way that would make her freely tell him everything. "The views in Minnesota are lovely too. I always liked watching the Mississippi River. It has a power you can see as it flows along. You know Austria sort of makes me think of Minnesota—it's green with lovely pine trees and the big river. It's interesting, many places in the world are similar," she said, watching him drive the car. He had such a way with the big machine, making it do just as he pleased, making it look so easy to drive along the bumpy roads of the country.

"I'd agree. So many places are similar, but each has its own difference. Do you miss anything specific about your home?"

"I miss my family and people I know the most."

"Tell me about them," he said, keeping his eyes on the road as they went around the vineyards.

"I think I'm still suffering from the unexpected death of my mother about two years ago. She was my rock. I'm sorry she was so against my marrying Goff," she began to confess, not realizing this is the information he didn't want to know and she didn't want to tell him now—later for sure, but now, all of a sudden, it was out.

"You're married?" Heinrich almost gulped. Had he lost her with these few words? The only chance for his future, was it gone?

"I was. I'm divorced. It's not every day you're going to meet a divorced woman, but that's the truth. I put all the blame on myself," she said, looking at his profile, trying not to see the expression on his face. She knew he most likely wouldn't want to be involved with her now, a divorced woman. What would his peers say? What would society think?

Heinrich stopped the car. He sat there behind the steering wheel, speechless, truly thrown for a loop for that moment. He took a couple of deep breaths, trying to give himself time to think. He couldn't seem to adjust to the words "I'm divorced." Finally, "I'm so sorry" slowly came out of his mouth.

Helen wondered what "I'm sorry" meant? Was he sorry she was divorced, or was he sorry for being with her? What was his next move? Was this the last she'd ever see of him? If it came to it, she'd release him from her heart, but it wouldn't be easy. She'd do whatever he needed.

She continued, "It was my fault. We married too quickly and had a baby ten months later. He was in the navy, then deployed into that terrible war. It was very difficult for me to live with my mother-in-law. She never liked me because, to her, theater people were at the bottom of life's people, probably underneath thieves and murderers. It was amazing to me anyone could be so uncompromising about another person's work, not giving them a chance to show their quality, but jumping feet first into assumption. I wasn't a floozy. I came home at night. I didn't go off with other men. I didn't have a 'bad actress' reputation, but I was an actress and a good one.

It's interesting how some people are born to be something. I was born to be an actress, to entertain people."

The count listened as he started up the car. He found himself understanding what she was saying without letting any kind or religious or moral ideas beat on him, telling him to put her aside and find someone else. For him there was no one else. He admired the fact she'd told him of her past. He wasn't naive and knew very well that situations often dictate what people do.

"What happened between you and your husband?" he asked, looking at her for a second.

"We had a nice life, other than his mother putting herself into our life. He came from a fairly wealthy family but never aspired to be wealthy. He was contented with little, but I needed more, and with a baby, we needed more. I realized the theater work in Minneapolis and St. Paul wouldn't be enough. It was then I was cast in a movie. If I really wanted the opportunity, it meant I had to go to Hollywood, to leave Betty and St. Paul. It was a very hard decision finding the best place for Betty. Finally I left her with the woman who lives across the hall from us, thinking when the filming was over I'd be back again to be a mother to my little girl. When the film was finished, I was cast in another film, then another until I found myself here. I guess I didn't love Goff enough. I needed the films, the work, the money, and the prestige they gave. When Goff returned from the war, he divorced me. I deserved it, I know, but I couldn't stop the theater in my blood. You remember, I'm sure, that Renoir couldn't stop painting, and even with a terrible case of arthritis he strapped his paintbrush to his hand and worked on. That's what it was for me. I couldn't stop."

Heinrich listened as he'd never listened before. What she said made sense. She seemed to be a strong-minded woman, one who could take care of herself. She was the kind of woman he needed to support him and to work with him. He admired her honesty.

"You have a little girl. Tell me about her," he said, wondering what this fact would bring to their relationship.

"Yes. Her name is Betty Gray. She's just about the sweetest baby anyone could want. She's beautiful with big blue saucer-type eyes that look straight out at you, melting your heart. She's got medium-brown hair and very cute feet and hands. I love feeling her hand when she reaches out to touch my face. Babies have the softest skin, and they have a magnificent smell. I don't know exactly how to tell you what they smell like. Maybe it's spring, but whatever it is, it's wonderful. She's a charmer. She makes me smile just to think of her sweetness. She's going to be a lovely adult," Helen gushed.

"My, my. She sounds perfect," he said, changing gears as he turned the car around a corner.

"She is," is all her mother could say.

He smiled. He began to wonder how much of a hold little Betty Gray had on her. Would she jump up in a flash and go running back to St. Paul if something should happen? Would she be able to truly leave all that behind and truly start a new life with him?

"Are you sure you feel all right about the people who are taking care of her now?"

"Oh, yes. Betty is in very good hands. I have every confidence she'll take good care of her until I get back." Helen smiled.

"I'm glad you have such confidence. She's also got her father's parents there in St. Paul," he said, wishing he could look at her to see her reaction while he put the car into another gear.

"I didn't want them to have her! They'll tell her horrid lies about me. No! She's best where she is!" Helen could feel a tear forming in her eye. She knew Harriet would take care of things. Slowly the tear rolled down her cheek. When Heinrich saw it, he realized she loved her child very much. He pulled off to the side of the road, putting the car in neutral. He leaned over, put his arm around her, and gently stroked her face.

"Oh, Heinrich. I hope I haven't done the wrong thing," she wept but quickly snapped out of it. She knew Betty was in the best hands. Maybe they weren't family hands, but they were good hands.

"Everything will be all right, don't worry," he told her.

She looked into his royal eyes. They kissed, and as they did so, she put her arms tightly around him. He pulled her close, letting him experience her softness, her perfume, and her being. There in his arms she made this lonely man feel important, more so than the country or his royal position ever had. He gently wiped away her tears with his index finger and kissed her again on the cheek, tasting the saltiness of the tears' remaining moisture. He was in love, and he was glad. Child or not, divorced or not, it didn't matter. He'd begun to truly live.

That kiss led to another and another, each one becoming more passionate. Heinrich couldn't believe the moment. He'd never kissed any woman as he was kissing Helen, and he'd never received such beautiful, sex-filled kisses back. She woke his senses, making him more determined to have her, not only as his lover but maybe as his wife. He realized the things she'd just told him were important, maybe life altering, but they weren't going to change how he felt and what he wanted to do. He needed her. He wanted her and all that seemed to go with her.

She pushed back a little, wanting to see the expression on his face. He was smiling. There was such a lovely twinkle in his eyes, but it was the way he smiled that told her everything—that age and status didn't matter.

I wish I'd met you first, she thought but finally said instead, "You make me happy."

"I do? You're sure?" he said.

"Oh, yes, for sure."

He smiled. Finally love had come to him, the kind he'd wanted, the kind he needed, and the kind that would sustain him for the rest of his life. He put the car in gear, driving it back on to the road. There was such a wonderful feeling of forward motion; it was the way their lives seemed to be going. The moon was high off to the left, letting Helen see his profile. She loved his look of pride and pleasure. He was a fascinating man to watch and think about. All that he did amazed her.

"How's the film going? I'd love to come to visit the set again someday," he all of a sudden asked, watching out for a large hole in the road. *I have to have someone out here to fix that*, he thought.

"The film is progressing well, at least I think it is. I haven't seen any of the daily runs, and the way films are made it's hard to know how much of it is finished."

"You could never run a country like that, but sometimes, with a repeal for this or that or an amendment added here and there, I guess the process is similar." He smiled, adding. "Always striving for what is best."

"I suppose so. Things of quality take time."

"That's true."

The night was full of promise and had been an important moment for them. Helen's love was growing by the moment. He wasn't anything like Goff. He was paced, planned, careful, and responsible—all the things Goff wasn't. She was tired of Goff's whims that sometimes took them to people she didn't like and knew had no respect for her. He'd let her do theater but never supported her in it. He came to opening night and closing night, but what he did in between he never said. She assumed he wasn't home alone but at his mother's being fed and drilled by her. The thing that took her heart was that Heinrich was the opposite of Goff. She first realized how much she took things for granted. Life with Goff was sometimes moment to moment, but with Heinrich things were steady. She could count on him doing something, not just anything. Not only that, but life with Heinrich would be comfortable and directed. She wouldn't have to worry about money again. It was a nice thought. He was the crown and felt she was the jewel in it. The love she felt for him was made up of the extreme respect she had for who he was and what he did. She admired his intelligence but felt a little awkward, for she knew her knowledge was beneath his.

"Are you free to come to the set day after tomorrow?"

"I will be," he said. "I'll make sure."

"I'll get permission for you tomorrow. I'll be so happy and proud to have you there."

He smiled. People didn't tell him they would be happy to have him around, much less proud to have him involved. She was something new, and he was amazed.

She added, "Do you want to know anything else about me?"

"Not now. I'm just happy being here with you."

"Me too, but if there is more needed, I'll tell you."

"I know, darling. Thank you."

"I love driving these hills of Vienna. Even at night it is fascinating. Heinrich, do I see a deer there?"

"I think you do."

"I hope the car won't scare it."

"It probably will. I just hope it doesn't jump out onto the road and into us. They look gentle but can be dangerous. No, it looks as if it is going deeper into the brush. Good." He kind of sighed.

As they drove near Helen's hotel, the air was different than in the woods—heavier, more humid. They watched the hotel lights twinkle as they approached, driving up to the front entrance. It was a welcoming place. Heinrich was proud of the capital and that it made such an open statement of friendship and diplomacy.

He parked the Daimler. Getting out, he escorted her to the front door and into the lobby. He wanted to take her in his arms and kiss her good night so badly, but his own protocol wouldn't let him, so they just held hands and then said good night softly. He watched as she went up the stairs and disappeared around the corner to her room. Driving back to the palace, he thought of all she'd told him. It was good, and day after tomorrow, he'd get to go to the set and see her work.

The night didn't speed by for either of them. They each kept remembering the evening, playing it over and over in their heads, enhancing each special moment.

The next day on set, Helen asked if the count could come to see the shoot.

"He's absolutely fascinated by moviemaking," she told Herr Rubin.

"I can't see why he shouldn't come. He has to be quiet and not take up your time," he said a little sternly.

They know. They absolutely know of my friendship with him. Is it a problem? I hope not. I'll let Heinrich know they are suspicious. Gossip travels, and I don't want any problems for him, she thought as she heard Herr Rubins agree.

"Helen, could you come for makeup now?" Herr Schmidt asked.

"I'll be right there," she said, smiling. In a sense this was beginning to be fun. How many other girls get to have a secret romance? Who cared if they knew of her and Heinrich? She just didn't want them to use it to promote the film.

Chapter 14

That day's filming went well. Everyone was pleased, especially the director who was beginning to get nervous about the shoot schedule. He didn't want to be over budget. His growing reputation was based on it. By the time Helen got back to the hotel, she found Heinrich waiting for her in the lobby with a glass of Mosel and a plate full of Munster cheese and salami cut into the thinnest possible slices the kitchen could make. It was paired with small round rye buns in little pretzel shapes.

"Frau Leveroos," he quietly called her name, standing up and gesturing for her to come and join him. She looked so beautiful and young. As she drew near him, he could see the fatigue of the day on her face, but her eyes sparkled as she saw him, and then came a big smile.

"You are like a breath of fresh air to me," she said, reaching out to take his outstretched hand. "It's been a very long day."

"My dear darling Helen. I'm so happy to see you. Are you sure this filming isn't too much?" he quietly asked, looking at her and wanting to take her into his arms and kiss her.

"Sometimes I think it is, but to see you brings my spirit back."

"What a kind thing to say," he said, not knowing how she really felt or of the attention she needed. "It is what it is."

"Come and sit down. I've got a glass of Mosel and some food for you." Taking his hand, he led her to the small table in the corner.

The moment Heinrich took her hand, Helen felt magical, and the magician was leading her to the source of life: food and drink. He still seemed like a fairy tale. Girls from Minnesota don't date or even know counts, but here she was doing just that.

"Heinrich, this is wonderful. Thank you." She looked at him, realizing how lovely it was when a man made such thoughtful gestures. He'd made her heart forget all other men she'd met before him. He was just so very nice, kind, understanding, and encouraging, but did he want something of her? She began to wonder if possibly she was being chosen to promote Austria through her work in film, as a remembered presence from her work in films. How could she do that? She was an American and knew nothing of diplomacy or promoting a country, particularly one with such an important history. If he should ask such a thing of her, how would she be able to do it? Of course she'd say yes, but could she do what he wanted? Everything looked so beautiful; the wine sparkled in the glasses, the food looked so tempting, and Heinrich had a special look—inviting, open, and irresistible. Helen, at that moment, would have gone to the moon for him, but she was glad to settle there at the table with him, letting him wine and dine her.

Taking her glass in hand, she toasted him. "Prost." He smiled, also toasting her. As they sat there, he began to tell her of Austria, first a little of its history and then some of his ideas for the future. She began to realize how very much he loved the country and how he wanted, through his guidance, things to go well.

"Helen, I want this future to include you," he said as he looked over at her while she sipped the last drops of wine in her glass. He poured her another while refreshing his own.

"What do you mean? I have this film to finish, and then I'll go back."

"If you were my wife you wouldn't have to go back," he said, smiling.

He surprised himself at the abruptness of the statement. He hadn't thought about marrying now, but there was something about her that made him realize she was the one he'd waited for. Of all the women he'd known, she was the first to open up the door of his desire and passion, releasing them and exposing him to what life was really all about. She made him want to live the rest of his life with her and for them to produce a family. The few others he'd known hadn't touched his heart. Finally she'd come.

"That's true. Please give me a little time to consider what all this could mean for me and Betty Gray." She was completely unprepared for the moment, overwhelmed. Never in her wildest dreams had she thought he would propose. Now what? Could she really become a part of Austria and, in this way, as the wife to one of the county's royalty? The possibility began to set in.

"That's fair. I'm offering a radical change to you. It will take a bit to grasp it, but, Helen, you would be wonderful for me, not to mention Austria. I love you."

"Heinrich, can you or the country could deal with someone such as me? I'm divorced, and I'm fairly well-known in film and the theater. What will the church say? I don't want to bring embarrassment or problems," she said, almost beginning to cry at the possible outcome. Heinrich didn't deserve all that. She wanted him to be happy.

"It doesn't matter. I don't see why any of that will matter. What you do now is very similar to what you'll be doing later. You are going to melt everyone's heart, as you have mine." He smiled.

"I will? I love you. I've made up my mind. I can't wait to be Mrs. Harrisch," she said. "Countess," he corrected.

"Countess? It sounds so strange to me. I'm the luckiest girl in the world. I can hardly wait. How, when, where?" she asked.

"Darling Helen, I'd like for us to marry as soon as possible. This coming fall would be nice, September or October," he suggested.

"I'd like that too. The fall is always such a pretty time of the year, and it's not too hot."

"That's true. Let me see if the city hall is free around that time. What about the twentieth of September? Would that be too soon for you?"

"The twentieth would be perfect or thereabout."

"The next thing I must do is ask the church if they are free then. Then I have to get the license and form an invitation list. Is there anyone you want to invite?"

"The only people I know here are Herr Rubin and the cast and crew of the film. You know I have caught bits and pieces of information, actually gossip, about us from them. It is a close society, and it's hard to keep secrets. I even overheard them betting on us," she said, starting to laugh.

"Well, let's include all of them. I'd like to have a reception at the Grand Hotel after the ceremony, since this is turning into a large event, but it is what it should be—guests, good food, wine, and music."

"The way you do things, I am sure it will be all of that."

"Well, we do have to give our friends what they want, throwing a little of what we want in there too."

"Speaking of the people, is there something done for them on such occasions?"

"Not in our case. If I was emperor there would be a state wedding. Family and dignitaries from all over the world would come, but since I'm a count, it will be much more private. We're pretty much free."

"Good. I'm sure I could carry off a grand state affair, but I'm glad we don't have to."

"Everything is going to be just fine and done as we want."

"I can hardly wait. I think everything should be left up to you, including inviting Herr Rubin and the cast and crew," she said, smiling.

The feeling of butterflies she gave him was new, but this jittery sensation also put him on cloud nine. He was amazed he felt so young in her company. How was it that she was able to open him up, giving him a different frame of mind? She turned on a new light in his lonesome heart, bringing his love to an all-consuming passion, a sensation he'd never known. He wondered if all men in love felt it and hoped they did. All of a sudden he was glad he wasn't a prince, that he could marry her without any strong scrutiny from the members of the government or church. If any questions were to be asked by someone higher, he would satisfy that interest by revealing what needed to be known.

It took a month to get all the details in place, as Helen did her best encouraging him, even to the point of suggesting he also invite a number of family and friends he hadn't thought of. Heinrich was delighted with this idea. He was also truly amazed at what had to be done and the red tape involved just to get married.

All of a sudden, becoming a countess, a person of royalty, made Helen think of being an American. The whole aristocracy thing was so unnatural, making her fearful of this upcoming life.

Would she be able to represent Heinrich correctly? She wasn't trained for European life, plus she was quickly beginning to realize what she would have to face. She'd have to give up her American life, her citizenship, her career, life on the stage; but as she thought about Heinrich, dear Heinrich and the reason she'd come to Europe, things began to fall into place. She wanted him, to live with him, to work with him, and, most of all, to be his wife.

"Thank you, darling. No one pours a glass of wine like you," he said one evening as they sat in his room discussing the day while waiting for dinner to be served.

"I've always been good at pouring things and spilling things too." She slightly laughed.

"I am too." He paused and then continued, "Your birth certificate will be needed. Do you have it?"

"No, I'll have to write to the city hall in Stillwater for it."

"Please write tomorrow."

"All right I will," she answered, adding, "Heinrich, have you invited the priest's mother and his grandmother? I understand she is seventy-eight. I'm sure the old lady would love to be included," Helen suggested.

"What a lovely idea, but they are already included. It is so nice of you to think of them though." He looked at her, seeing the kindness of her heart, adding, "The invitations will be hand delivered to each of them."

"Who will give me away?"

"How about my friend Hans Von Mannersdorf? You've met him."

"All right," she agreed, "He seems like such a good person."

"He is. I'm sure he'll be happy to accept. I know he likes you."

"I'm glad," she said, looking at her glass, and then at him, adding "You really have some good people around. Are you asking him tomorrow?"

"Yes. The sooner the better. I'm glad the important thing is finished. Shall we go into dinner?"

She finished the last of her wine as he held out his hand, pulling her up gently.

"I'm starved. Let's," she said, standing in front of him, gently kissing his cheek.

Eating the dinner consisting of several of Austria's national dishes, Helen again wondered what she was supposed to do as countess. She wanted to know the role, exactly what her duty was, her obligation. She wanted to make Heinrich happy, but what was a countess supposed to do? Strangely enough, she didn't seem to mind that her career as an actress was dwindling, the cause of which is what led her to Europe in the first place—her age. She was very satisfied with the work she'd done but knew it would be no match for the work she would be doing for the man she loved and her new home.

As they ate, Betty Gray came to Helen's mind but stayed there only for a moment. Everything in that area was in the past. Betty was fine, safe, and happy. The Careys were her life along with Kevin MacArthur, Helen hoped.

Chapter 15

October 16 was a beautiful fall day. Its vivid colors made everything kind of glow. At the door she welcomed the best man, Hans Von Mannersdorf, who looked so tall and proud wearing his national dress. Helen wondered if Heinrich would wear the same. Hans beamed at seeing her, and he knew that Heinrich would be so proud and happy when he saw her in her dress, a long satin creation with a sweeping skirt overlaid with elegant lace. The bodice had a dramatic but respective décolleté not covered in lace as the skirt. She had a two-row pearl necklace, which hung down almost to her breast, and a white silk rose penned at the top of her décolleté. Her hair was done up in a style similar to that of Empress Elizabeth. Helen looked and felt like a countess as she accepted the bridal bouquet from Hans, which was traditionally given by the best man. The roses in the arrangement perfectly matched the silk rose on her dress. It was perfect. She was ready.

Entering the city hall, she wondered where Heinrich was. Was he as disappointed as she was about divorced people not being allowed to marry in the church? But here she was at the lovely city hall and about to marry the most wonderful man, her Heinrich. This place was, for her, more wonderful than any church. Then she saw her friends, the cast, and crew all decked out in their finest. She smiled, waving to them. Finally she saw Heinrich. He looked so regal, tall, and elegant in his formal attire. Her heart did a little pitter-patter when she saw him come to her in that wonderful suit.

He could feel his love for her glowing, almost tingling, as he smiled back. At that moment he realized his real life was about to begin. Not that the work of a count wasn't real, but it didn't make his life full. Now marriage to Helen would make everything complete, as it should be.

Somehow his mind's eye could hear a child's laughter. Were they going to have a baby? He hoped so. Life was good.

They came together, standing in front of the magistrate, both listening to what was said. In a flash it was over, each agreeing of their own free will to be married to the other. The next moment everyone was congratulating them and saying, as they headed out the door to the reception, they'd see them at the Grand Hotel.

The Grand Hotel waited with pride, as another royal would be coming to celebrate something that was important. Feeling it was part of his job as best man, Hans had come earlier in the day to make sure everything was in place. He loved this old hotel, the style, the charm, especially the way it made him feel. He knew Heinrich also loved the place. He remembered their mothers often had afternoon tea together there. Being older now, he marveled at that friendship and how it endured for so many years. He wished the two old ladies could have been with them today.

Proudly walking into the hotel with Helen, his bride, on his arm, Heinrich smiled like a child at Christmas. He felt he was the envy of everyone in Austria at that moment.

"Welcome, Count and Countess Harrisch. Congratulations on your marriage," the hotel manager greeted them.

"Thank you very much," Heinrich answered, looking at the man. He had known him for years and always appreciated his attention. Especially his attention to details and remembering certain things.

The manager smiled, replying, "It's my pleasure. I hope you'll find everything to your liking this evening."

"I'm sure we will," the count replied as he escorted Helen into the large dining room.

As always the room was beautifully elegant with its light-pink and white walls, painted with small bouquets of edelweiss intertwined between strands of gold ribbons and ivy, showing off the flowers. It had been decided to serve the guests buffet style, after the champagne was offered. Hans offered the first toast of the evening, simply saying he was very happy Heinrich had met Helen, and he was glad he was safely married, which brought a laugh from those around. He then went on to welcome Helen into her new life. Helen blushed a little as everyone applauded. She looked over at her new husband and blew him a kiss. He sent one back. This toast brought many others, each wishing them all the happiness in the world. People began to gather at the buffet table, eyeing the fabulous array of food presented. The chef had outdone himself, especially with the large chafing dish filled with hot dogs and another with American potato salad. Still others were filled with American mustard and ketchup and hot dog buns.

The novelty food was enjoyed by everyone, especially after a small demonstration of how to create the perfect hot dog as given by the chef.

The reception lasted longer than planned. Finally when the last guest left, Heinrich sat down on one of the side couches and sighed a huge gasping sigh. Helen came over collapsing beside him.

"I don't remember getting married was so tiring. Maybe I didn't notice because I was younger," she seriously joked.

"Let's not do it again anytime soon," he said, wishing he could take his shoes off, adding "Are you ready to go back home?"

"Yes, very much. I loved every minute of it. Thank you. Everything couldn't have been better, more beautiful, or more fun. Oh, Heinrich, I am now going to yell out loud how much I love you."

Raising her voice, she started, "I love Heinrich Harrisch, the most wonderful man in the world."

"Oh, you, what am I going to do with you?" he said, laughing while gathering her into his arms and kissing her deeply.

Hearing the commotion, the hotel staff had come to see if everything was all right. They smiled at seeing the first kiss.

Chapter 16

The next morning they came downstairs. The night bed brought such excitement, passion, and sleeplessness, letting the early morning slide into late morning without either of them noticing. Walking into the dining room, they were greeted by gentle applause from the small staff. The bride and groom smiled as they took their seats. Heinrich was hungry. He was delighted to see the eggs, ham, rye rolls, tea, and coffee waiting. His staff had done a better job than that of the hotel. He was proud of them.

"What looks good to you, darling?"

Looking over the offerings she said, "Look, we have tea too. Everything looks wonderful.

Look at the fabulous fruit bowl. I'd like some of it."

"We're a couple of gourmets."

Sitting down at her new regular place in her new home, she said, "We are. Darling, I'm afraid to say, but the film isn't quite finished. There's a few more days of shooting to be done. Two weeks from now the scene in the garden is to be reshot. It shouldn't take too long. Then three days later the scene at the riverbank and then the scene at the market."

"All right. I'll stay home and keep things going," he almost complained like a child who'd been left behind.

"Heinrich, I'm sorry."

"It's all right, but I'll miss you."

"That's so sweet. I'll be back soon."

"I'll have things ready for a lovely evening, waiting for you."

"I'm looking forward to it. I'm sorry, but that's show business."

The morning of the reshoot, it was hard for her to leave the passion of the night and their wonderfully warm bed.

"Heinrich, you just stay there and rest."

"I can't. I want to be with you. I'm going to get some coffee for us and some of those rolls I like. Come to the dining room when you're ready."

"That sounds wonderful. I'm hungry. You know I seem to be hungrier than normal. I guess it's married life," she said, starting to dress.

"Me too," he agreed, adding, "I guess so."

As Helen dressed, Heinrich got things ready. It really wasn't his forte, but in a pinch he could carry even this off. Soon Frau Kaiser, the housekeeper, came and finished setting up the dining room. The delightful smell of fresh coffee brought Helen down. She was pleased to find such a beautifully set table.

"That's what I need, thank you." She quickly drank some coffee and buttered a roll, eating it before she got to the door. The cab she'd called last night stood out front waiting. Off it took her to the days ahead of filming. Heinrich was worried he'd be lonesome and bored, but he understood.

As she said, that's show business.

The reshoot went fairly smoothly. It took a bit of getting used to the new changes. Helen couldn't believe things were so different. New ways of camera work and blocking confused her, but it felt good to work on the film again. To be on set and mingle with the cast and crew. They were all so interesting. She was fascinated by the new things the crew did. She'd actually forgotten all the work they went through so the make-believe magic could come to life. The atmosphere made her realize that she still loved acting, bringing characters to life, and all that went with it. A quick thought of how she had missed it went scurrying right through her brain. It was wonderful being with actors again. They just seemed to make her pulse race faster, but it was different. Was it the people or was it her? Soon it would all be over, and she knew she'd miss things, but it wasn't enough to pull her back into that life. It was just enough to remind her of the past. Heinrich had several important events he was expected to attend yearly—the flower show in Vienna, the children's fair, and the yearly dog show. He particularly liked the dog show, such fun. He loved dogs, always had. He thought back on the day his mother had said yes to his having his own dog. It was a little female wire-haired fox terrier, very similar to King Edward VII's Caesar, but much prettier. He'd loved little Vickie, whom he had named after King Edward's mother, Queen Victoria, and when Vickie died Heinrich never wanted another.

Heinrich, being a sentimental person, was proud that he remembered, without staff help, birthdays, anniversaries, church holidays, and other events. He felt they all needed to be remembered if one wanted tradition.

For him it was tradition that bound the present to the past. *Did Helen's family have traditions?* he wondered. *What did they do for Christmas or Easter or any other holiday?* He'd have to ask her about it.

The days Helen was away, Heinrich had no problem finding something or someone to revisit. His new life with Helen took all the time he, earlier, would have spent with family and friends. Now, the fourth day of the shoot, he decided he'd go back and ask his cousin Frederich to lunch with him at his club. He wanted to know about his trip to America and understand fully why Frederich couldn't come to the wedding. His handwritten note was sent by courier. An hour later, Frederich's acceptance came. Heinrich dressed, put on his driving hat, coat, and deerskin gloves and then drove the mile and a half to his club. There, near the doorway, Frederich stood beside his new Renault, waiting. They shook hands and then embraced.

"Good to see you. It's been a long time. I'm glad you could come on such short notice. Let's go in."

"Truly good to see you," Frederich said, seeing Heinrich's familiar face.

The club looked the same to Frederich. He hadn't been there in years.

He remembered how the entrance seemed—clublike, not like a government building or some sort of store but offering a feeling of something solidly special. He felt relaxed as he stepped into the large entrance area with its elegant yellow-and-black tiled floors, white double doors with big round door levers leading into the reception room with a large, long mahogany bar and mirrored background displaying all kinds of bottles of wine and liquor. There were two stained glass windows on each side of the bar, one female form depicting morning and the other evening. He remembered wishing years ago for these two glass ladies to be real. That was before he'd met, married, and lost Sylvia, his wife of only five years. Tomorrow would be the fifteenth anniversary of her death. As the years went by, he never found another woman that completely attracted or called to him. He wasn't depressed or unhappy; there were just too many things to do. Now the two cousins were together again.

"Here's to life," Frederich toasted, raising his glass toward Heinrich.

"Here, here," he answered, clicking his cousin's glass. Good crystal always makes such a nice ring—bell toned and expensive sounding when clicked with another of its kind.

"I'm so happy since I met Helen. She has made me young and alive again. What was I thinking all those years, and what was I doing?" he asked himself.

"Doing your part for the state kept you busy and your own interests."

"That's right, but it wasn't enough. I'm lucky."

"What are you doing now?" Frederich asked, unbuttoning the top button of his jacket.

"I'm waiting for Helen to come home. She's an actress, or was an actress. She's off doing a refilming of something she was in earlier. Just a small section."

"An actress. My, you've hit pay dirt. My, my."

"Frederich, she's not that kind of actress or woman. She was in the theater because she had a talent for acting. She has a good memory. She also looks very good on stage and is quite believable," Heinrich boasted.

"I'm glad you're happy."

"I am. She has changed my life totally. I even want to have a child with her."

"My, my," Frederich said again. He didn't know quite what to do with this piece of information.

"Yes. I wish we could have twenty."

"Twenty!"

"You know what I mean."

"Start with one and then see what happens," he said, pausing. "You know today is the fifteenth anniversary of Sylvia's death. Fifteen years. I just can't believe she's been gone for so long, and I don't have any children to carry on my line," Frederich said, looking down. "It was sad and lonely being wifeless and childless."

"It's interesting you never found anyone else."

"Well, there was one, but well, it's a long story, not for here and now," Frederich said, giving a little smile. He took a long sip from the cognac glass in front of him, inhaling its essence, and then sighed.

"I'm sorry it didn't work out."

"Me too, I think. She turned out not to be the person I thought she was," Frederich said.

"Good thing you realized it before it was too late."

"Yes." He sighed again, but this time it was a quick remembrance of relief.

"What are you doing now?"

"I'm still working on a new automobile engine. I'm sure I can create something that can go faster than thirty kilometers per hour, but maybe I should put my time into designing better roads."

"Now that's a worthy project," Heinrich said, looking straight at him. "I'll think on it, but I would love to drive fifty or more."

"It sounds dangerous but fun." Heinrich laughed a little.

"It is on both accounts." He paused. "I'm going to visit Sylvia's grave this afternoon. Would you like to come with me?" Frederich asked, changing the subject as he thought about the white and red roses he'd buy for her when he left the club.

"I'd like that, yes," Heinrich said.

"We can walk the mile or so to the cemetery. Pay our respects then come back for supper at the new hotel. I've heard they serve wonderful food," Frederich suggested.

How could Heinrich say no? This was turning out to be a nice day. The waiter was signaled and the bill paid. They slowly walked to the cemetery, enjoying the pleasure of each other's company. For a moment there was a bit of remorse in Frederich's heart, for he was truly enjoying his time on the anniversary of the worst day of his life.

Walking into the cemetery, they pushed open one of the huge, heavy black wrought-iron gates. Its squeaking loudly spoke of serious neglect. As with many old cemeteries, the grass was uncut and grew over ankle length. The graves themselves stood as proud remembrances of people no longer here. Some stood erect; others leaned over with the burden of time.

"It's just over here around the Schmidt monument." Stepping near the plot, Frederich took the flowers out of the white paper they were wrapped in. He bent over, gently laying them on top of Sylvia's lovely marker of black marble, matching all the others that announced the people buried there. He was glad none of the markers were tilted or had fallen over onto the ground. He'd paid the cemetery people every year to make sure these stones were properly standing. It had been money well spent. He then got down on his knees, said a quick prayer, and kissed the stone with her name and dates.

Heinrich said a prayer as he watched Frederich. Death was such a terribly permanent thing, affecting both of them, but in different ways. As he turned away and backed toward the cemetery entrance, Heinrich was glad he'd come along. He remembered Sylvia as a pretty woman with lovely auburn hair, brown eyes, and a delightful smile. She didn't need to be a beauty to be beautiful; in fact he sort of feared beautiful or very good-looking women. They were so often false, hurting his heart, and then abandoning him. For that second he thought about Helen. She was beautiful and solid in her convictions. Her beauty was not the kind of legends. It was genuine, comforting, and sweet, letting his eyes know as he looked at her that she was there to stay.

As they left the cemetery it was the first time Frederich felt easy about leaving. So often, completely devastated, he could hardly tear himself away. But now there were so many things that took his interest, giving him back his passion. He began to realize his time of mourning was over. He'd always loved Sylvia, but now a new faster automobile engine called him, and the roads for it needed to be designed. In the back of his mind, he had the idea to get in touch with the Benz Company to see their progress. Possibly they could use some of his thoughts on the subjects.

As they walked the mile back toward town, they came across a small tavern. Its charming facade lured them in. Once inside, again the wonderful smell of Austrian cuisine led them to a table. A pretty young waitress, dressed in a charming blue dirndl, came to take their order. Both wanted steins of dark beer and an appetizer of cheese and sausage. She left menus with them, which they quickly looked over. Heinrich has had a serious love affair with Wiener schnitzel his whole life, so it was chosen without thought. Tonight they were offering a caper sauce, which sounded like a nice idea, along with a rindsuppe to start things off. Frederich easily agreed. Twenty minutes later the men sat with big plates of their favorite food in front of them. The time rushed by as they talked, ate, drank, and relished every second of the time spent together. This was living.

It was nine o'clock when they reached their cars. By the time Heinrich got home he was tired. It had been a long but very good day. Now his bed called him. Tomorrow he would write to Carl Benz at the Benz Company to inquire about setting up a meeting with them to discuss some of his ideas, but most importantly, Helen would be back. She'd been gone, it seemed, forever; and he could hardly wait to put his arms around her, kiss, and love her.

The night was long. All that food brought on a terrible indigestion. He'd had this pain before, but only once. This time he thought it would kill him. He realized he needed to see someone about it. The next morning he was pain free. Completely forgetting about the pain of last night, he sat down to write the letter to the Benz Company; but first he reread all the material he had about Carl Benz, trying to decide the best way to approach him. He began the letter.

Next he wanted to pick up Helen, but he didn't know where the filming was being done, so he puttered around the house, waiting for her to arrive. Watering the indoor plants, taking his dog Spot for a walk, getting some glasses and a bottle of her favorite wine ready, putting it in the morning room, and then going out to mail the letter to the Benz Company occupied his morning wait.

Fifteen minutes after he got back, she arrived. Opening the door, he smiled, pulled her in, and kissed her, saying, "I've missed you so much."

She found his response a little funny, but she was very glad to be back. "Darling, come, sit down. Come into the morning room. I've got a little something ready."

"I'm so glad to be back here. Everything looks wonderful and the same. Oh, Spot. Come here. How's my beautiful dog? I've missed you both so," she gushed.

Heinrich opened the bottle of wine and poured each a glass. He said, "I don't like it when you're away."

"It won't happen again," she said, taking the glass as she sweetly kissed his cheek.

"This house is like a mausoleum without you. Do you know how dark it is at night? Now tell me all about the filming."

"It was fine, but I realized it is not for me anymore," she said, sitting down. Her eyes looked at him with a twinge, realizing that things now were better.

"What happened?"

"I was so glad to be on set again, but everything was so different. Has it really been that long since I did the shoot? One thing I was most surprised about was that Herr Michael Gross, my husband in the film, seemed so much older and was. Apparently he'd been ill and it showed. He seemed old, not the man of earlier. Illness and the train wreck he'd been in affected him a lot. He just wasn't the same person."

"My goodness, how sad," Heinrich said, taking a sip of wine.

"He had a lot of trouble doing his lines. He somehow seemed lost," she said with a quiet tone of voice.

"Does he have a family to look after him?"

"Yes, his oldest son now lives in Washington DC. His second son is in Vienna studying medicine, and his daughter is married and doesn't have time for him. I felt so sorry for him I almost brought him home with me."

"I'm glad you didn't," Heinrich said, starting to pour another glass of wine for himself, thinking, *She really wouldn't do that, would she?*

"It just all seemed so different. I see it is not where I belong anymore, but yet I still have a passion for it. This industry, if I can use that word for it, is on the move. It's modernizing fast."

"I would think that's a good thing."

"It is, just that I'm left behind."

Heinrich was glad she felt left behind. He wanted her here, with him, not off filming some movie somewhere away from him.

"Circumstances change, people change, advances happen. It's the natural way of things, darling," he said, looking at her. He loved the way she looked. Her hair shone like satin. Her eyes called to him. He felt she was more beautiful than she was before she left.

"You're right, but why so quickly?"

"I don't know, darling. Modern times with progressive ideas. Everything is moving forward," he philosophized. "Let me refill your glass."

"Yes, that's what I need. I love the wine you've chosen. Have we had it before?"

"Yes. We have several more bottles down in the basement."

"Somehow it tastes so much better. I can't believe I've forgotten."

"I doubt you've forgotten. You're just in a different frame of mind."

"You're probably right. I'm so happy to be back." She smiled at him.

He'd do anything for her and knew it was the same for her.

"Frau Kastenmier sent a note to you. It's on the table in the study."

"I'll get it later. Right now I just want to kiss and sit beside you. I've missed you, darling. I've missed you," she said. She put her arms around his neck and kissed him.

He put his arms around her waist and pulled her close. Her clothes were soft but formal, not letting him truly feel her body. He stroked her cheek and kissed her again.

"I can never get enough of you," he said, smelling her perfume. It made him realize only she could bring him worthiness.

"How could I have been so lucky to have you? What did I do that was so good that brought you to me?"

"Fate, beautiful fate," he said.

She gently released herself from his embrace, stood up, took a deep breath, and said, "You take my breath away."

He brought his hand to his lips and said, "You see, I love you."

"And I love you," she said, turning toward the study, wondering what Frau Kastenmier could be writing about.

"How did you fare without me?"

"It was tough, but I did have a chance to visit some friends and family. I spent a whole day with Frederich. He had some interesting things to say about his trip to America. He's got himself a very fancy new Renault. His wife Sylvia died fifteen years ago. Where does the time go?"

"My goodness. Did he ever marry again?"

"No, he's put his life into working on a gasoline engine that can go faster than thirty kilometers per hour. He's also thinking about designing better roads."

"Now that's something we could all use."

"I agree. You know, going to the cemetery was difficult. Seeing all those names of family etched on stone markers is really a sad thing, but I'm glad we went. On the way back we stopped for dinner, and I had some of the best Wiener schnitzel of my life. That cook is a master. This morning I looked up all I could find about Carl Benz and wrote him a little about my ideas."

"I'm very glad you had such a productive time. For me it was a trip down memory lane. I realized that part of my life is truly over. I felt out of place there," she said, this time with a sigh.

"Maybe it's for the best, darling. You have other things to do now," he said, grateful that she didn't fall back into wanting to be in films.

"You're right, but I'm glad the changes were made. It's a nice film, and I'm glad to be a part of it."

"I'm proud of you and your work. Movies give people pleasure."

"Yes," she said, opening Frau Kastenmier's letter, asking her to work with her for the Children's Sport and Games Charity in the fall. The letter looked old school, making Helen remember her grandmother in St. Paul.

Chapter 17

The University of Minnesota's Halloween party came just in time, giving relief from the terrible study hall troll who seemed to be eating Betty and everyone else up daily.

The party would free her from the work that almost began to feel like an albatross around her neck. That morning she wrote a few pages of the newest English assignment. Around noon she washed and set her hair, later pressed her dress, and slowly got ready, wondering about the party. About seven thirty Mary Jane, the girl across the hall, picked her up, and off they went arm in arm, giggling with excitement. The lights of the gym were low, kind of spooky. The scent of burning candles and some strange Halloween sounds, made by the janitors and one of the kitchen staff, easily suggested Halloween dread and excitement. The local band played popular songs and kids danced. A nice table decorated with a black tablecloth with sandwiches and punch sat fairly close to the door.

"Betty, I see Tess Jones over there. Mind if I go talk to her for a bit?" Mary Jane asked.

"Not at all," Betty answered. She turned to go toward the music, when all of a sudden she stood face to face with Kevin MacArthur.

"Betty, fancy meeting you here. Hi," he said, truly happy to see her again.

"Kevin, it's nice to see you. Nice party," she said, thinking about how good-looking he was. She hadn't forgotten.

"Yes. Would you like a glass of punch? They've got some funny punch that's smoking. It's green."

"Okay. I'll be game."

They walked over to the smoking dark-green punch, each drinking two glasses.

"Do you feel different?" he asked jokingly. "No."

"Neither do I. Would you like to dance?" he asked. "Yes," she said, disregarding what Mollie said earlier.

The minute Betty put her hand in Kevin's and her arm on his shoulder, it felt familiar. He still fit her when they started to dance. The music and beat of that samba, with its melodic sound, made them feel right. It was fun.

"Have you seen Summer Powell lately? I haven't seen her in ages." Betty asked.

"No, she's got a new boyfriend. Brad something."

"Good. Brad and Summer sound like a nice combination," Betty said thinking that maybe she and Kevin could be together.

"I still remember that lovely party at your house. I'll never forget the wonderful food as long as I live."

"It was a nice party. I'm glad Summer brought you."

She tried not to listen but felt shards of her mother's words going through her brain.

"Now we're at another," he said, remembering the elegance of the other event.

"Yes. How are your classes going?" she said, changing the subject. "Fine. Italian is kind of hard, math is so-so, and geology really isn't my thing. I'm having the most fun in acting class. The history of theater is fascinating. We've started working on a special Eugene O'Neill piece."

"Eugene O'Neill is a good writer. He makes people think."

"He sure does," Kevin said, adding, "He's making me work."

"It's good for you. If you want to be an actor you have to work," she teased him, smiling.

"Let's keep dancing. I don't want to work," he said, pulling her closer, bringing her almost up to his eye level. She had lovely gray-blue eyes, which he thought told him he was more than alright. There was a look of softness about her hair, which made him think of early fall breezes, scattering browning oak leaves hither and yon. He knew there was something special about Betty. She had the gift of intelligence without being stuck up or boring, and she had a way of making one feel they were the only one and all she wanted to do was to see or hear them. It was genuine. It was this that Kevin really liked about her.

Three dances later, Joan Schappe tapped Kevin on the shoulder, interrupting them. Betty stood there as Joan waltzed him away. It was all right. Five minutes later he was back, asking for another dance. They danced nearly every one. They felt good together, letting their affections grow. If only Mollie wasn't so against actors, Irish Catholic actors.

They began to spend good times together, studying, working on his lines, going for walks. One Sunday afternoon they even had time to make a snowman in front of the dean's house. Classes went well for both of them, and when the Christmas holidays came, Betty asked if Kevin could join them for Christmas Day lunch. Mollie couldn't say no. She really wanted to know what this Kevin was all about. Sadly Mollie only knew what she felt was the bad actor, Catholic part. It was time to find out some of his good points.

On December 21, Mollie had things ready for the holidays. The gifts were bought and wrapped, the Christmas Eve party was arranged, and Mrs. Malroy was free to come help and serve for two days. This year she asked Mrs. Malroy if her niece Liza could come and help with the party. Mrs. Malroy wanted this girl to go into domestic service. She thought this party would be a good introduction. Liza had had some boyfriend trouble and was trying to stay out of his way, and Minneapolis was a good place to hide and learn.

Mollie and Betty put the last touches on the buffet table. Everything was so beautifully Christmas.

"Mother, you should have been an interior decorator," she said as she sat down before getting dressed.

"It would have been fun, but as you know, I was too busy taking care of your father. Before the guests come, do tell me about Kevin."

"What do you want to know?"

"Well, who are his people? How long has his family been in the States? Does he have brothers and sisters? What does he like?"

"Kevin is one of the nicest men I know. As you know, he's very handsome. He loves the theater and is a really good actor. He has asked me to help him with a special Eugene O'Neill piece for his exam. I love listening to him do the lines. He's so believable, and the way he does the lines almost brings me to tears. There is so much feeling there. I envy him, being able to remember like that. Kevin says O'Neill makes him work. The more we do the lines, the more he brings O'Neill's work to life. It's amazing."

"Tell me about his family," Mollie said.

"He's got an older sister, Terry, who's taking a lot of courses in literature. Kevin thinks she wants to be a novelist."

"That's unusual."

"I think so too," Betty agreed.

"Can she make a living writing?"

"Probably. I hope so for her sake," Betty answered.

"What else is there about Kevin?"

"He's had a very sad childhood. His parents died when he was only four."

"What happened?"

"I don't know. He didn't go into any details."

"That's very sad. Loss of family is one of the hardest things one can go through," Mollie said, remembering losing her own children.

"I would agree."

At that the doorbell rang. Mrs. Malroy answered it. The first of thirty-five guests arrived. Kevin stood there proud as a new penny. He smiled as he saw Betty come to the door.

"Come in. Where is your friend Lila?"

"Her father came to town just for the day, so she went to dinner with him. She sends her apologies."

"I'm sorry she couldn't come, but I understand," Betty said, secretly glad he came alone, adding, "Come in and say hello to Mother."

Betty took his hat and coat and gave them to Mrs. Malroy, who put them in the closet. She then brought Kevin over to see Mollie.

"Good evening, Mrs. Carey," he said, extending his hand and looking around the large living room.

Mollie looked at him and smiled. She was impressed.

"Good evening. Do sit down and tell me about yourself," she said, shaking his hand, with her full attention on him.

"Thank you. Betty has been such a nice friend. I've asked her to help me with the play I'm in," Kevin said.

"Betty has told me you're studying acting and theater."

"Yes, I love it. I'd like to become a professional actor," he said, feeling a little under the gun.

"Do you have a backup plan, in case acting doesn't work out?" Mollie asked.

"I could teach," he said, beginning to wonder about the older lady.

"Oh, that's a good idea," she said, thinking that teaching would never clothe Betty. Why didn't he try business? She began to wonder, sorry that he was wasting his time. "Mr. MacArthur, may I offer you a beer or some ginger ale?"

"Yes, please. A beer."

"Betty, would you get Mr. MacArthur a beer?"

"All right. What about you, Mother?"

"I'll have the same." Usually Mollie only had beer on very hot days, but she wanted to share this experience with handsome Kevin.

"Have you lived in Minneapolis long?" he asked?.

"We've been here twenty and some years. My family came back east from Montana. Originally, after leaving Scotland, they arrived to Pennsylvania then went to Montana. We still have some cousins in the Livingston area."

"Oh, that's quite a history."

"It was quite a life. I do love going back to visit the ranch, but Minneapolis is my home," Mollie said, sipping the beer Betty had brought them.

"I like Minneapolis too," Kevin agreed, looking at Betty. "The university has opened up many possible choices, but theater is my main interest. It's becoming a passion!"

"I hope you'll do well."

"Thank you." He smiled at her. "I'll try. I feel I can."

"Betty is interested in English and writing," Mollie said.

"Writing is fun. It lets one gossip about people without being reprimanded for it. Your pen is free to let your mind spill out lots of things you'd never say out loud to anyone," Betty said.

"I can see that. I'm just now thinking of O'Neill," he said.

"I'd love to be able to write like him," Betty said, sighing a little with desire.

"A lot of people would," Mollie said sipping, the now-less-foamy brew. "They say a writer has to suffer to bring out emotion. I wonder if it's true," he said, thinking about it for a moment, adding, "I don't think my sister has suffered much except for the death of our parents, but she does have a different personality. I was four when our parents died," he said, expecting the usual sentences of sympathy to come from Mrs. Carey. "What took them?" Mollie asked, sorry for him.

"They died in the terrible flu epidemic of 1918." This horrible fact still hurt him as though hot coals were being thrown into his heart.

"Oh, Mr. MacArthur, that is just awful. I'm so sorry," Mollie said with true pity in her voice.

"It was. I don't remember them that well. It's probably easier that way, but I do miss not ever having had them."

"How old was your sister?"

"Terry was seven. I think she's always been affected by their deaths."

"What happened to you two? Who took care of you?"

"We were raised by my father's parents in Minneapolis, until they couldn't take care of us anymore, then we went to an aunt and uncle."

"You were lucky to have so much family who were able to take you in."

"Well, that's a matter of opinion. It was hard on us to deal with old people. I know our grandparents loved us or tried to. After their deaths, we went to our aunt and uncle, but they really didn't want us and couldn't afford us. Their hearts were in the right place, taking us out of Christian responsibility since there was no one else."

"Again I say I'm sorry, but you were lucky you didn't end up in an orphanage or, worse yet, some workhouse."

"Thank God. I wish I could have my parents around now. I want them, especially Mother, to know what I'm doing and studying. I'd like to find out from her where my interests come from," Kevin said, looking at Mrs. Carey, his blue eyes wide open, meeting hers.

"I wish you could have that too. I can't imagine what it would be like not to have parents," she said, her feelings about actors softening.

"Death really is a thief," Kevin said, looking at her. He wasn't sorry he'd told Mrs. Carey part of his life, especially due to the way he felt about Betty. He was lucky. His childhood had been hard, but he'd survived and prospered.

"That's true. Everyone is visited by that unwelcome intruder, but life goes on, and here we are," Mollie said, liking his intelligent statement.

"That's a good way of looking at it," Kevin agreed.

She noticed he seemed to have a true sense of being for one so young. It was refreshing to meet someone who was willing to express their history so openly to an almost stranger.

As Mollie and Kevin talked, Betty liked the way her mother was listening to him. She could see Mollie was slightly smiling and nodding. Could she have changed her mind about this dislike she'd had of the Irish? It was beginning to look like it, or was it all for show?

"Pardon, madam, the guests are arriving," Mrs. Malroy came in to announce.

"Thank you."

Mollie got herself near the door as the first guests arrived, momentarily leaving Kevin's story. The Carsons, and then the Blakes, the Smiths, the Johnsons, the Websters, the Nelsons, and, lastly, Angela Strem all arrived at once, kind of like a swarm of bees filling the house with buzzing chatter. At eleven o'clock everyone had left, and Mollie and Betty sat in the living room with their third glass of wine, relaxing.

"It was so much fun. I loved every second of it."

"Me too. Did you see how people seemed to be drawn to our friend Kevin?"

"He talked theater. I guess no one knows anything about it. He certainly had them right there," she said, tapping the palm of her hand.

"He did, he really did. I think I'm going upstairs now. It's been a long day. Thank you, Betty dear, for all you did tonight, playing second hostess."

"It was fun, Mother, and a big success."

"I think so too."

"Sweet dreams," Betty said, kissing her mother gently on her cheek. "You too."

Both Betty and Mollie went to bed happy. For Mollie it was another feather in her social bonnet, and for Betty the amazing part had been seeing Mollie putting away her prejudice and letting Kevin come into her circle. Betty knew Mollie liked him—who wouldn't like him? A little nagging thought went through her brain as to what Mollie had said earlier. Mollie was a woman of conviction and wouldn't just toss out her beliefs. Kevin was not yet in the bosom of Mollie's family. This would take some doing.

Chapter 18

Mollie woke up the next morning with thoughts of the fun of last night's party singing in her heart. It had been wonderful seeing everyone again. They all seemed so well, but she was worried about Sally Carson. Something was amiss, but not a word of anything wrong was said. She hoped she'd just imagined something and most likely there was nothing there.

Betty came into Mollie's room and, as she often did, got on the bed and hugged Mollie good morning.

"Morning, my sweet girl."

"Morning, Mother. I think we had a big success last night," Betty said, smiling at her mother.

"I think so. I didn't get to tell you but Angela Strem has invited us for coffee at her shop this afternoon."

"That's unusual. I don't remember being invited for coffee before," Betty said, looking at her mother.

"It is, but I think Angela is somewhat lonely."

"Maybe we should take her out to dinner tonight," Betty suggested. "It will give me a chance to wear that lovely blue dress I got there last year."

"That, my girl, is a lovely idea. I'll call and suggest it." Mollie smiled at the thought that Betty was so kind.

Fifteen minutes later, Mollie called upstairs to Betty, who'd just finished washing her face, with the news that Angela had accepted. She was delighted to be invited to dinner. Every day she worked long hours in the shop, and this invitation had come just at a time she needed a little boost.

That morning Betty worked on a poetry assignment as Mollie puttered around the house, watering the plants, reading the newspaper, and asking Mrs. Malroy if she would make a vegetable soup for that day's lunch.

It was four thirty when they rang the Strem Studio bell. Mrs. Strem's assistant answered, happily letting them in, sitting them down into the salon, decorated in true Austrian Empire style. Mollie found herself looking at the picture of Emperor Franz Joseph and another of his gorgeous wife Elizabeth stationed on the wall opposite the door. They were such interesting and beautiful people, the emperor, in his full military dress, and the empress, in her beautiful royal gown, seemed to look down at her with majestic silence.

Already seated in the salon was a somewhat middle-aged lady. There were several dresses laid out on a table beside her. They smiled at each other. Miss Strem had a lovely orange Hungarian Herend Apponyi china coffee service for six sitting on a larger table in the middle of the room. It sat on a lovely large porcelain tray, which matched the pot, cups, sugar bowl, and cream pitcher. A strong smell of coffee emanated from the coffee pot.

"Hello. Welcome, Miss. Carey," Angela said, coming through the curtain barrier separating the back salon from the more formal front salon. She walked to Mollie and shook both their hands.

"It's so nice to see you. Thank you for the wonderful invitation. I must admit I'm very glad to be away from the business for a while."

I thought we needed a little more time together," Mollie said, looking at the other lady sitting across the room, smiling at her.

"Countess Harrisch, may I introduce Mrs. Carey," Angela said, continuing to smile. "We've been special friends since I opened my salon back in 1920."

Mollie smiled at the countess. She had a look about her Mollie liked. She'd never met anyone of royalty before.

"I'm pleased to meet you," the countess said, extending her hand. "I'm happy to meet you too." Mollie looked at the elegant woman dressed in dark green and smiled.

Mollie liked this lady's style and that she was a countess. How often does one meet a countess?

"Countess Harrisch has recently come to Minneapolis," Angela said.

"What brings you to our fair city?" Mollie asked, noticing the way her hat sat on her head in kind of a theatrical way.

"I've returned because I've recently become widowed. My husband passed away four months ago. I began to feel it was time to come back to the Midwest. There was really nothing keeping me in Vienna except memories and Heinrich's estate, which I have given to our nephew."

"Certainly you have lots of friends there."

"The people we knew were mostly people Heinrich knew. Business and official people. I have many friends too, but I want a break, some fresh air," she explained.

"I understand. When my husband Frank died, I sort of felt the same," Mollie sympathized.

"Being a widow isn't easy."

"I agree. My daughter has helped me so very much. I don't know what I would do without her," Mollie said.

"I'm a bit envious," the countess said.

"I'm sorry. I hope you find a new happiness. It will take time," Mollie offered.

"I'm sure so." The countess looked down. Heinrich was so dear; she could feel a tear starting to form. The days were long without him and the nights even longer. She wasn't sure what to do with her life now.

"Life can be very unfair, but time is a healer."

"They say so. I know it's true. I'm lucky I have several projects to take my mind off things. I sponsor several children's charities here, and I'd like to visit them. I'm thinking of doing some sort of fund-raising for them. When, I don't know. Right now it's just a thought."

"That's very interesting, Countess Harrisch," Mollie said, smiling at the lady.

"Angela thought this was such a gallant idea." She'd often heard of important and famous people sponsoring such things but had never known of any of them actually coming in to do something.

"I'm also in the market to buy a house here in Minneapolis. It's such a pretty place. I'd like to be here. I have one in Los Angeles, but it is so far away from what real life is. I don't like Hollywood anymore," the countess told them.

Mollie looked at the countess, wondering how anyone would have houses in so many places, or could say specifically they didn't like Hollywood. What did Hollywood have to do with anything? She was impressed with what she thought was the lack of aristocratic attitude. She'd imagined someone like that wouldn't talk to ordinary people. Now here they were talking of houses and life. She liked the countess.

"I would really like to do something while I am getting established." She loved the Austrian style Angela gave to the salon. She almost thought she could hear the gentle flow of Strauss's music.

"Would you like to join me for the Arts Board meeting this coming Thursday?"

"I'd like that very much." Helen smiled. She was glad an opportunity came so quickly.

"May I pick you up? The meeting starts at 1:00 p.m."

"That would be wonderful. I'm staying at the Depot Hotel."
"Yes, I know it."
"Lovely."
"Countess, do you take sugar in your coffee?" Angela asked.
"A little and some milk, please."
"And you, Mrs. Carey?" Angela asked, looking at Mollie.
"The same please."

Angela smiled. Coffee hadn't been served to anyone for a long time nor had there been such good company. For this moment, the past was safely in the past. The letter telling of Franz's sister's death was momentarily put there too.

As Angela's thoughts were partially on that letter, Mollie wondered about the countess. But only for a moment. There were other things of importance now, like this year's new designs and color and finding out what Angela had been doing lately.

Chapter 19

Helen couldn't hide her fears of being discovered. They came racing to her. Did Mrs. Carey possibly recognize her from the old photo? Why had she given it when she gave up Betty? Quickly she took several sips of coffee to calm her worry. Mrs. Carey was never to know who she was, nor did she want to upset anyone's life, especially Betty's. Yet she wanted to know Betty, about her, not as a mother but as a friend, a friend of a friend. In case their paths might finally really cross, she realized she needed to tread lightly, to preserve the delicate beginning of her new life.

"Countess, have you any fund-raising ideas? If I may I would like to suggest a fashion show, sometime in the future," Mollie offered.

"That's a very interesting idea. I'll think about it. Maybe," Helen answered, looking at Angela and around the lovely shop. Looking around the shop, she noticed a number of photos nearby; and one alone on a chest of drawers near the curtains intrigued her so much she couldn't stop looking at it. She began to wonder if Betty would look like that now, all grown up. A twinge came, biting her feelings of guilt. This young woman had a distinctive hairline like Goff and what she thought would be the shape of his nose. Could this photo be of Betty? She twinged again. She wanted to ask who it was but didn't.

As Helen looked at the pictures, her ear caught the music coming from the radio. She was sure it was an aria from Bellini's *Norma*.

"I first heard this magnificent piece in Vienna. It stirs me every time I hear it. It's as though God wrote it, not man," the countess said, remembering the first time Heinrich took her to see *Norma*. The evening just sparkled and the music lingered in her mind for days.

"I agree it is wonderful and deep. It makes me feel something, but the music I really love is Strauss's *Fledermaus*. It's fun and funny at the same time," Mollie said.

"Fledermaus is romantic and fun, but for me the most passionate must be from Verdi's *Don Carlos* aria O Don Fatale, which seems to fit my life at times," the countess said.

Betty and Mollie looked at each other, wondering what the countess could have meant by this. They realized they hadn't had enough time with her to know what her history was.

The subject changed when Mollie spotted a yellow sweater she thought would look good on Betty. She asked Angela to wrap it up while finishing the last drop of coffee in her cup.

Paying for the sweater, Mollie noticed the hour. "Oh my goodness, look at the time. I really should be getting home."

"I so enjoyed this time together. Thank you for coming. I'm looking forward to seeing you again."

"You both are so nice to help me with my cause." Helen truly smiled with happiness. This day was much more than she ever thought, especially with the possibility of seeing the girl she thought might be Betty.

As Mollie left, the countess watched Angela go to the front of the shop with Mrs. Carey. She came back a moment later.

"Countess, please do tell me what happened to Heinrich. I just can't believe he's gone. The last time he wrote he said he was in perfect health."

"I'd been away for a few days, and when I came back he seemed fine. During my absence he told me he'd had a wonderful time visiting with his brother, having dinners, talking about cars and about life. They had a wonderful time together. During the evening I got back, we drank some wonderful Mosel, as I listened to him tell me about things. When he went to the basement for another bottle, out of the blue, he suddenly collapsed. He'd died by the time the ambulance came. I still can't get over it. It is like a bad black dream," she said, her voice almost breaking at having to repeat the story again. "I didn't know you knew him."

"I'm so sorry. I knew him, actually about him, through my father who worked with him years ago. I'm glad you're here now. Are you going to stay long? Have you any plans?"

"The main thing is, for the moment, to get back on track."

"I hope I can help," Angela offered.

"You already have." She smiled at her.

"I'm glad."

"Heinrich was so wonderful, a beautiful human being. He was older, but I never cared. He was very community driven with ideas for better streets, better services, and better land use. He loved cars and particularly the idea of them going faster. He had a mechanic mind in that respect. He came from a very distinguished family. It is interesting to know, four hundred years ago, before the founding of America, his family obtained a huge land grant from Leopold II of Austria for bravery during military services rendered back then, and the title. As a result, they became very wealthy. Naturally, with sound management, the family's wealth grew and continues to do so now."

Angela nodded, remembering the Harrisch family's achievements.

"I was his only wife. It's interesting a man could be married to something other than a woman. In that sense Heinrich was married to Austria. She was his first and biggest love, but I never felt in second place. His sense of duty was remarkable. He loved all the functions he had to do for the state, and he never got tired of the job or bored with the daily duties. He loved it all. It's what fueled him," the countess said proudly.

"I'm very sure you both had such a good life."

"Yes, we did. He was so sweet so often. He always gave me the most beautiful gifts, many times, just because, saying he still couldn't believe I'd married him. I always thought this was a little strange because that's how I felt too. He brought much-needed balance to my life." She smiled a sweet remembering smile.

Chapter 20

Betty walked in the door of 2530 West Lake of the Isles Boulevard a few minutes after Mollie arrived home.

"Mother, hi. How was your day with Angela?"

"It was, my sweet girl, very interesting. I think it is time to have a Pink Lady," Mollie suggested. "Do you remember how to make them?"

"I think so," Betty said, going to the kitchen. "Mother, why don't you wait for me in the living room. I see the mail is on the table in the front hall."

"Okay," she said, going to the front hall to see if the mailman brought anything interesting. "Bill, bill, advertising. Nothing I want to deal with now," she said.

"Here you are, Mother," Betty said, coming into the pretty but somewhat formal room, offering one of the cocktails.

"Thank you, dear. Today at Angela's was most interesting. I met a very nice lady there. Believe it or not, she's a countess," Mollie said, sipping her drink. "Betty dear, you are master of this drink. Just perfect."

"Thank you. A countess of what?" Betty asked, raising her glass to clink with Mollie's.

"She's Austrian. Actually she's American but married an Austrian count."

"That's interesting."

"She recently lost her husband. There is some kind of sadness about her. She doesn't look sad, but you can feel it," Mollie told Betty.

"I'm sorry. Is she nice?"

"Yes, very nice and pretty. She told us she once lived in Hollywood and had a big house there but became disinterested in it."

"That's interesting. Does Angela know this? I wonder why she was in Los Angeles."

"I don't know, she didn't say," Mollie answered. "She does seem sort of lonely. Kind of pensive. Maybe there's some kind of regret there."

"That's too bad. How old do you think she is?" Betty asked, sipping her drink.

"It's hard to tell with women. I'm going to guess forty and some, probably less. She was wearing a dramatic dark-green dress with red trim around the neck and the end of her sleeves. It looked tailored and very expensive."

"She sounds special," Betty said.

"She also had a very interesting hat. Her outfit reminded me of something from the movies or the stage."

"That's different."

"I thought so too. She told me she's back here because she didn't want to be alone in Austria without her husband."

"That's sad too. I'm sorry." Betty said, looking at Mollie who seemed to be thinking two thoughts at once. Her face got a special look when she did that, halfway between a frown and a slight smile. "How long ago did he die?" Betty continued.

"Four months ago, she said. I sympathized with her by telling her your father also died recently. It is an unusual thing to have in common. Not that being a widow is unusual but that we are both recent widows."

"Did she say anything more about her husband?"

"No, she did say something sad. That the only things holding her in Vienna were memories. I guess she just wanted to be away from them," Mollie told her.

"I hope she's not running away from something," Betty said, wondering what her story was.

"I don't think she is. She doesn't seem like the kind of woman with a past."

"Now that would be something," Betty said, imagining something she could use in a future book.

"She also indicated she had friends, but most of the people she knew were business people and friends of her husband. It's not hard to see that she would have a lot of people in her life. They must have had an interesting life together. It's hard to imagine how they lived and what they did every day," Mollie said.

"It would be interesting to know. Maybe someday she'll tell us all about it," Betty mused.

"I will be glad to learn more about her." Mollie got a feeling the countess was needy. Not in things. There seemed to be something amiss with her. She seemed so alone. Mollie felt it wasn't anything about her husband. She felt she needed friendship, people, maybe even love. There were definitely a lot of questions about this woman.

"She sounds unique," Betty said.

"I'd agree. We should do something for her. Luncheon maybe."

"That's a very nice idea. When?"

"Maybe next week."

Chapter 21

That night Helen was aflutter about meeting Mollie. That they had come together after all the years. Mollie, Carey, Betty kept racing in her thoughts.

She seemed like such a nice lady, so different from me. How much is Betty like her? Maybe she's not. Do I truly want to know? Am I worried for nothing? She's such a sweet lady. Betty, Betty, you deserve better than me. Should I do something about it? Is this my one big chance? I need some time to think. Oh God.

These and other thoughts followed her into bed, not stopping as she tried to sleep.

It wasn't an awful night for Mollie. She was charmed by the countess and anxious to show off Betty at the upcoming luncheon. Plus, she was very sorry for the empty life the countess seemed to have now. A nice little luncheon would be a good thing. Something subtle, not ostentatious, just lunch with the girls.

The next morning Mollie made tea and set the table with the regular tablecloth made by Gracie for her and Frank's wedding. Offerings that morning were fresh hard rolls, butter, jam, and fresh cottage cheese.

Betty came bouncing in with her usual youthful energy. "Morning, Mother. Mother, this is a lovely breakfast. Oh, did I tell you about the spring class trip?"

"No. What's it all about? When and where?" Mollie asked, buttering part of a roll she'd broken in half.

"The class has decided we should all go to California, to Los Angeles."

"Oh, that's interesting."

"I think so too. The weather should be good."

"Not only that, Los Angeles is a very interesting place. I almost envy you," Mollie said, sipping the Earl Grey tea she'd made.

"Can I go?"

"Of course. You should see it. I hope you'll get to go to Hollywood too, to see the film studios and maybe see some of the homes of the movie stars. Oh, I'd love to see John Wayne's home."

"Mother, you're so funny. Shall I take a picture of it for you?"

"Yes, please do," Mollie replied, taking a bite of cottage cheese on her plate.

"Okay. I will, if we get there. I've heard there are tours taking people around to see the stars' homes. But we have a private tour inside three stars' homes."

"That sounds wonderful. I'm sure you'll have a marvelous time."

"Kevin is also going."

"Mr. MacArthur? I'm sure he'll have a lot to see and learn there," Mollie said, still not sure of his Irish connections.

"I know seeing one or two of the film studios will be part of things," Betty said, happy she could go on the trip.

"When is the trip?"

"It will be the first week in April," Betty replied.

"For how long?"

"A week," said Betty.

"That's not too long. I should be able to survive, but it might be hard," Mollie kidded.

"Oh, Mother, you're so funny," Betty said, smiling at Mollie.

"Maybe I can get Gracie back here for that week," Mollie suggested.

Hearing this, Betty began to wonder if Mollie would be lonesome without her. She didn't want that. It would be a good idea if Gracie could come. They hadn't seen each other for some time.

"I think that would be a wonderful idea. You should write to her soon."

"I will. Maybe this afternoon."

Chapter 22

Two weeks later, Gracie's answer came. She couldn't wait to come see Mollie and Betty again, and something different. Her life in Montana, on the ranch, had been filled with feeding sons, a disloyal, arrogant, and now deceased husband, and isolation, but it was all she knew. Even though she had always been a little envious of Mollie, she loved her dearly. Their fathers, first cousins, had been fairly close, but not as much as these second cousins. They were more like sisters than cousins.

When Mollie married Frank and moved away to Minnesota, Gracie felt the pain of separation. No one was more delighted when Mollie and Frank got Betty. Shortly after, Gracie had her first son, Fred, and then two years later, Evert.

Two days after Gracie arrived, Betty left for the school trip to California. Both trips were uneventful. Gracie settled into Lake of the Isles Boulevard easily. The cousins were happy to be together again; Gracie loved being in the Midwest again. It was so very green with an almost forgotten feeling of things being close together and of things being on top of each other. She had forgotten how much fun Mollie was and how much fun Minneapolis was, not to mention Betty. Hearing of Betty's classes, Kevin, and of Betty's upcoming trip almost made Gracie's head spin. So much excitement in such a short time. Then it was just the two of them with lovely conversation over tea, of days long gone, walks around the lakes, trips to town, and meeting some of Mollie's friends. This was the gentle time Gracie needed and got.

Chapter 23

Once on the train, Betty found out Kevin's compartment was four down from hers. They spent the travel time watching the scenery, playing cards with some of the others, and eating. The plan was to go to the Brown Derby, Grauman's Chinese Theatre, and on a tour of the movie stars' homes.

The twenty-plus-hour trip brought them into Los Angeles about noon. The hotel had cars waiting to pick everyone up. Here they had the feeling of wide-open spaces. Everything looked so big, especially seeing the Pacific Ocean with its mighty roaring waves rolling onto the shore. Betty loved it all. The arid desert, brown cactus, and forced green spaces were an interesting change from the green grass and tall trees of Minneapolis.

That night they all walked around the area near the hotel. After Mrs. Diamond, the chaperone saw to it everyone had a room, and then they all had dinner together in the hotel dining room and then went off to bed.

The next day, everyone went on a tour that included Olivera Street to Sunset Boulevard, Hollywood and Vine. The browsed in all the stores, took photos of each other and others, and then had Mexican food from a street vendor. That night everyone went to Grauman's Chinese Theatre to see a William Powell and Myrna Loy film. Grauman's, as a very clever advertising move, got all the famous movie stars to leave an imprint of their hands and feet on the sidewalk in front of the theater. It was such a touristy thing to do but fun.

The next morning the bus picked everyone up for the private tour inside some stars' homes. They drove for an hour, up and down and around Beverly Hills, quickly seeing as they went to some very elegant, pretty, and big mansions. Of these, three were open for the group. The three homes open for the group were those of Billie Allen, Marian Swan, and Milford Timson.

"The one I really want to see is Marian Swan's house. She was such a wonderful actress. I must see hers," Kevin said with reverence and excitement. His dream was, one day, to get to know and work with her. She was his idol.

"I wonder whatever happened to Marian Swan. She just seemed to stop acting. No one has heard of her in years," said Betty. "I don't know if I want to see her house. Billie Allen and Milford Timson are enough for me," Betty answered at the thought of having to stomp through these self-glorified houses.

"Oh come on, Betty," he insisted.

The last on the list was Marian Swan's house. Just as the other two had been, it was a beautiful house—big and elegant with white stucco siding and a lovely garden around. There were four large palm trees in front. Like soldiers, they stood tall guarding the house. In the back was a screened-in porch, four-car garage, a swimming pool, and a tennis court.

They entered Marian's house through the front door. A white canvas path led them through the living room. Betty was surprised to see a white baby grand piano in the corner, against a gentle floral-papered wall.

"Kevin, look at that piano. I've never seen a white piano before."

"Me neither. It seems so Hollywood."

"Yes," the guide, a young woman, very tanned with long blonde curls and a tour guide badge pinned to her blouse, said. "It was used in New York for several Broadway plays and for several concerts at the met."

"My," Betty said, turning around to see it again.

"Follow me," the guide said.

White spiral columns marked the separation of the living room and dining room. The white dining room was decorated with a number of Wedgewood ceramics. From the dining room they entered the reading room. Betty was very impressed with the number of books Marian Swan had. She wondered if she read them all.

Upstairs housed six bedrooms. One had lovely chintz curtains with white flowers on corn-blue background with dramatically draped valences. This was called the blue room. The second was painted white but with yellow curtains and was called the yellow room; another had green curtains. The fourth and fifth rooms were locked, but the sixth room, Marian's bedroom, was painted yellow with lovely white drapes. On the wall between the windows were several rural prints. On an adjacent wall was a magnificent, long walnut dressing table with a large oval mirror and some pretty crystal powder boxes and perfume bottles. On the opposite wall was a lovely white-painted pine bed with an elegant bedspread matching the curtains. In the opposite corner was an almost decadent apricot satin love seat, with many little fancy pillows. An oval table stood beside it, holding several books of poetry. There was a matching chest of drawers beside it.

On the wall, close to the bed, was a painting of the Madonna holding the Christ Child.

"Notice the dressing table," the guide said. "I've been told this table was given to her as a gift from an admirer in France. The bed is a copy of one that was used in her last film."

She didn't mention anything about the prince or the picture of a woman holding a baby.

"Betty, look at the photo. I know I've seen it before," Kevin whispered.

When Betty looked at the photo she did somewhat recognize it. She looked again.

"I think I've seen it too. My goodness, it's me. It's the countess and me? How can that be? It's the same one I saw with Mother up in the attic one day when I was helping her find something for Gracie," she whispered. "Ma'am, the photo over there, can you tell me about it?" Betty asked the guide.

"Yes, of course," the eager guide said.

"Who is the child with Miss Swan?" Betty asked.

"It's an old photograph of Miss Swan and her niece."

"Oh," Betty said, smiling at the guide.

The guide smiled back. Many people had asked about the charming picture. The guide was sorry she didn't know who the child was and couldn't tell anyone.

Betty whispered to Kevin, "That's Countess Harrisch and me for sure."

"How can that be? Sure does look like the countess," he said.

"When I asked Mother about it, she said it was a picture of me and one of the girls who used to take care of me."

"How did it get here?" Kevin asked.

Betty began to wonder what Marian Swan had to do with her and Countess Harrisch. Had the countess been her nanny all those years ago before she became the countess? Who is Countess Harrisch? Who is Marian Swan? What did it mean?

Kevin had been so engrossed with touring the film studios he almost took notes of how things were done—cameras, lighting, sound stages—but he had noticed and commented on it.

Four days later they got back to Minneapolis. Betty was full of excitement and questions, wanting to ask and tell Mollie everything.

She'd bought Mollie a book about her favorite film star, John Wayne. Mollie loved it.

"Mother, may I invite Kevin over tonight?"

"Sure. I'd like to hear what he thought about Hollywood, since he wants to be an actor. How about for dinner? Shall we include Countess Harrisch? I haven't seen her for some time. I think she would enjoy you children."

"All right. There is so much to tell. We all had such an interesting time," Betty answered, not thinking that moment of the photo she'd seen a few days ago.

"I'm glad you did. I'll telephone Countess Harrisch in a bit."

Mollie smiled. She was always glad to have guests. It was the way the house was supposed to be, full of people.

Shortly after Betty went to class, Mollie phoned.

"Good morning, Countess Harrisch. This is Mollie Carey."

"Good morning. It's a lovely day."

"Yes, it is. I know it's short notice, but would you be free to join us for dinner this evening?" Mollie asked.

"I'd love to. What time?" the countess answered, happy about the opportunity to see them again.

"About six."

"Thank you, I'll see you then."

That evening Kevin arrived with a California spring in his step. He was glad to be invited to Betty's for anything. Just to be with her made him happy. This trip brought out the special feelings he had for her. He realized he loved her.

"Good evening, Mr. MacArthur," Mollie said as she opened the front door.

"Good evening, Mrs. Carey. Thank you for inviting me."

"It's our pleasure. I'm anxious to hear all about the trip. Betty has told me a lot of things. I wonder what your opinion is," Mollie said, looking straight at him, continuing, "Do come in. We're having cocktails in the living room."

"Wonderful. I had a great time. I think Betty did too," he said smiling. He was beginning to like Mrs. Carey. She was really very nice and an interesting woman.

"I'm glad. I think it was a good experience for both of you."

Kevin walked into the living room, looked over at Betty, and then sat down beside her. He gave her hand a little squeeze. She smiled at him and squeezed his hand back.

"Now tell me everything," Mollie said, offering Betty and Kevin a sidecar she'd made earlier.

"We really had a fabulous time. I was so glad to get to see the film studios, to see the process of filmmaking. We also went on an interesting tour of some of the movie stars' homes. Actually, only three were open, but they were all wonderful. I was also very surprised how hilly the area was. I never knew that."

"Tell me about the homes. Women always want to know about other people's houses," Mollie said with much interest, adding, "Cheers."

"Cheers," they said all at once.

"We saw Billie Allen's, Milford Timson's, and Marian Swan's houses. These houses really showed what money can buy. Swimming pools, tennis courts, long driveways, sometimes six bedrooms, huge dining rooms and living rooms. Some were too gaudy, too much show for me."

"Betty, whose house did you like best?" Mollie asked, taking a huge sip of her drink.

"They were all spectacular. I don't know which one I liked best. The strangest one was Marian Swan's," Betty said with a little smile.

"What was so different about hers?" Mollie asked.

"Well, first of all it was gorgeous, but she hasn't lived there in years."

"Really," Mollie said.

"Yes."

"Tell me about it."

"The house was fascinating, but what was unique was a very interesting photo."

"A photo?"

"Yes. An old photo."

"Why was it interesting?"

"Because I think it was a photo of the countess."

"Countess Harrisch? At Marian Swan's house?"

"Yes. She was holding a baby girl."

"That's fascinating," Mollie said as the doorbell rang.

Getting up to get the door, she smiled at Kevin. He was so handsome. She liked the way he seemed to treat Betty. She liked his manner of dress and the way he spoke, and she liked that Betty liked him. She wasn't sure in the beginning but now felt good about things between them.

She opened the door to Countess Harrisch, who stood there looking like a movie star in a lovely sea-blue silk dress with matching dyed shoes. She carried a pretty bouquet of flowers and a box of chocolates.

"Countess Harrisch. How lovely to see you. Please come in."

"Thank you. Please, a little token for tonight," she said, handing the flowers and chocolates to Mollie.

"What a treat. Thank you! I love flowers, and these are my favorite chocolates. How did you know?" Mollie almost gushed at the generosity but knew chocolates and other things were something the doctor said not to eat because of the heart condition they'd found earlier.

"I didn't. I'm very glad you like them." She smiled at Mollie. She was now very glad Betty ended up with Mollie.

There was a genuine sense of guilt lying underneath that brought out a feeling she never thought she'd have. She'd put Betty in a good place, but now that good place bore a hole in the center of her heart. She still knew Mollie had been the right place for Betty, and she was grateful to the woman.

"Come in. We're having sidecars in the living room. May I get you one?"

"Sounds lovely. Please," Helen said, walking into the large room. "Countess Harrisch, may I introduce my daughter Betty and her friend Kevin MacArthur."

"I'm pleased to meet both of you," Helen said, looking at Betty and Kevin. The mother factor began to scream in her head. She was now very sorry at what she'd done. How could she have given up her child for theater? As she looked at Betty, she saw Goff looking back. Again the pain of consciousness beat itself on her, and this time it included Goff.

The moment the countess sat down, Mollie gave her a cocktail. "How lovely. Thank you. Is this something new?" she said, trying not to think of Betty looking like Goff.

"I don't know. It's called a sidecar. So many new drinks are being invented now. Cheers," Mollie offered.

The previous subject changed. Everyone joined in.

"Delicious," the countess said.

"Countess Harrisch, have you known Mother long," Betty asked, studying the woman.

She had lovely eyes and a gentle face. Betty liked her look.

"Not too long. We met at Angela Strem's shop," she said, feeling isolated that Betty had just called Mollie "mother."

"I see," Betty said, looking at Kevin, who was looking at the countess, almost studying her.

"I've recently come back to Minneapolis. My husband died a while ago, so I decided to return home."

"You're from Minneapolis?" Kevin asked.

"Actually from St. Paul. I grew up there," she told them.

"I see." He was somewhat puzzled by the statement.

"What are you studying in school, Kevin?" she asked.

"Theater. I want to be an actor."

"That's interesting. One doesn't meet many young people studying acting." She smiled. "They say it's a hard profession and can be over quickly."

"I hope it won't be for me," he said.

"Me too." She smiled at him.

"And, Betty, what are you studying?"

"Literature and writing. I'd like to be a writer. I also ride, equestrian. I've won several ribbons and one cup."

"My, my. That's also very interesting," she said, already knowing from reading of it in the newspapers.

"What kind of things do you write?"

"I love poetry. I've done a fair amount. Just small pieces, but I would like to try a novel sometime."

"That's very ambitious. Do you have a plot in mind?" she continued the chitchat.

"No, but I want to make some sort of statement about life."

"I see. Isn't riding dangerous? Do be careful."

"I will. It can be, but I've got a very good horse. She's called Red Cloud. Countess, tell me about your life," Betty said.

"My life. Now that's a good question. What can I tell you? I grew up here. I went to school and met Count Harrisch when he was touring the States. We were married in Vienna. We did a lot of ceremonial things, opening bridges, highways, schools, and hospitals for the area. I was busy all the time."

"Do you have any children?" Betty asked.

"The count and I never had any children," the countess answered.

"I'm sorry," Betty said.

"Me too, but that is life."

"That's true," Betty answered.

"Tell me about your trip," the Countess suggested.

"It was very interesting. I liked California. I didn't realize it would be so different from here," Betty said.

"It is very different. It takes a bit of doing to get used to the climate and landscape. I felt the same," Countess Harrisch said, not realizing she'd confessed to having been in California. She felt very glad she was now in Minneapolis. For a brief moment she wondered what she should do with her house in California. One day she'd sell it.

As Kevin listened to the countess quickly speak of the West, he began to wonder why she'd been there and when. Vaguely she began to picture her in another place, as a younger person. Was his memory putting her in an old movie? Maybe one he'd seen as a class assignment. Could she have been in the early movies? Could it be possible.? He struggled for her name, but it didn't come. He let it go.

The meal that evening was one of the best everyone had ever had. Roast beef done to perfection, green beans with almonds and the cauliflower au gratin were just right, not to mention the endive and grapefruit salad with vinaigrette dressing. But the true star of the evening was the chocolate cake with chocolate icing that nearly put Kevin in a state of nirvana, making him ask for and get a second piece. After dinner they went into the living room where Mollie served coffee and liqueurs.

"Mrs. Carey, what a delightful meal. My waist doesn't let me eat like this very often. What a treat," the countess said.

"Thank you. I'm glad you enjoyed it," Mollie said at the countess's mention of her waistline.

"Do you have any baby pictures of Betty? I'd love to see some," the countess surprised herself by asking, never having a thought she would ask such a question of Mrs. Carey.

"I do. We have a nice selection in the library. I was just working on putting some new photos in an album yesterday. Would you like to see them?"

"I'd love to."

"Why don't we leave the young people for a bit and finish our coffee in the library?" Mollie suggested. She loved the way Betty photographed. It didn't seem to matter at what angle. She looked good, especially the ones by her favorite photographer in Chicago. He had a way with the camera that made everyone look like royalty.

Kevin stood up as the ladies picked up their coffees and headed to the library. As they left, he seated himself beside Betty.

"Gee, the dinner was good. I think I'd marry your mother for that cake," he said, almost not joking about the dessert and Mollie. He liked her, finding her fun and charming.

"My, you did like it," Betty chuckled.

"Not as much as I like you," he said, looking at her. He reached over, taking her hand in his. "Betty, I love you."

Betty was silent. This was unexpected. Oh, she liked him, really liked him. Now he'd broken the ice. She smiled the biggest smile she'd ever had. Yes, she loved him too. She leaned toward him, and he put his arms around her neck. They kissed. A sweet, gentle long kiss. Then another.

"More cake," is all Betty could dreamily say.

"No, thanks." He smiled and then released her. He couldn't believe he'd actually kissed her. Not just a peck on the cheek but really kissed her, and she kissed him back.

Mollie and the countess walked slowly back to the library. Mollie then, by habit, looked back toward the buffet table in the dining room to see if there were more plates to offer more cake. She saw the kiss and smiled to herself. This fellow really wasn't so bad, and he was good-looking, but the problem of him being Catholic still remained. She wondered what else he had that would disappoint them. She didn't want Betty hurt. Betty had a sad experience when she was seventeen when her boyfriend, some Phil, left her for a pretty blonde named Kay Delbro. Mollie never like the name Kay after that, or Phil. She then decided nothing mattered—Catholic, actor, or something else. Now wasn't the time to think of such things.

As they went into the library, Mollie said, "Countess, you'll have to excuse the mess in this room. As I mentioned I was looking at and trying to put some more pictures in the album. Photography is such a wonderful thing."

"I agree. What do you have here?"

Mollie piled several albums on the side table. The countess's heart pounded with anticipation, enthusiasm, and fear as Mollie opened the first album. The countess quietly gasped at seeing Betty as she'd been when she left her. Again she thought of how much Betty looked like Goff, and again a pang of remorse came.

They spent at least a half hour enjoying the pictures. With each one, Mollie had an interesting comment as the countess questioned where it was taken and when.

"Betty was such a charming child. I'm amazed at those photos of her riding and jumping. Did she ever fall off or get hurt?"

"She didn't fall off and, thank heaven, never got hurt."

"That's good. Is this your husband with her?" the countess asked, trying not to say "her father," whom she knew was Goff.

"Yes. They were thick as thieves. I am so sorry he died when she was so young. She still carries him in her heart and often speaks of Daddy."

"That's nice. I can imagine it must have been hard, but she has you."

"I'm the grateful one. She adds so much to my days. I'll be sorry when she gets married and goes off." She paused. "But that is the natural way of things."

"That's true," the countess agreed.

"It's amazing how fast they grow up. Drinking from baby bottles and dragging dolls around to first kisses. All within the wink of an eye. I saw Kevin kiss Betty a bit ago," Mollie confessed to something she didn't like. She hadn't had enough time with Betty, and now she was afraid this young man might take her away.

"They kissed—well, I guess it's normal. She is such a pretty girl," the countess heard herself saying.

"I suppose it is, but I don't think it's good for her to be mixed up with an actor."

"Actors oftentimes do have the tendency to be unreliable," Helen said, remembering. "Movie magazines are always printing things about adultery or stars being poor parents. Possibly the most important thing to actors is their career," she said, knowing, adding, "I guess artists are different in that everything has to be done for their career and about promoting themselves."

"My goodness, I would never be able to live in such a way. Everything about a career, never," Mollie flatly said.

"It has everything to do with ego. Their careers come first, before friends, family, and life."

"Countess, you speak as if you know."

"I've only heard," she said secretly, crossing her fingers in the lie.

"Oh, to change the subject, Betty has started on her first novel," Mollie boasted.

"My goodness. How exciting. What's it about?"

"I don't know. I think it has something to do with the West," Mollie said. "She hasn't given me any details."

"That's wonderful." Helen was very impressed with Betty's art—to start a book. She was very proud.

The lunch ended with Kevin saying he had to go and study. A big exam was scheduled for Tuesday. Mollie was saddened this broke up the party, but school was school.

Chapter 24

The next afternoon, Kevin was tired of studying and memorizing. He'd read it all several times over and felt good about what he knew. Now coffee at the Old Mill Lounge was in order. Once inside, he ordered the biggest coffee they offered, took it over to a table, and sipped it as he again went over in his mind the dialogue he needed to know. A moment later a gentle hand touched his shoulder. He looked up.

"Countess Harrisch."

"Hello Mr. MacArthur. May I join you?" she asked.

"Oh yes, please do," he said, pulling out a chair for her. "I'm glad you've joined me. I can't stop wondering if I have seen you before."

"I don't think so. I don't remember you from anywhere," she said, looking at him again.

"I know we haven't met but could I have seen you on screen?" he slowly asked, looking at her elegant dark-gray dress and matching hat, feeling surer than ever about the question.

"Why would you think that?" she asked, wondering what he would think of her if he knew of her past film and stage work.

"Because I was going through some old Howard Peck films for class, and well, you were quite a lovely woman and, well, a famous one."

"I'm feeling old but flattered you could have recognized me, but all of that were a thousand miles and a hundred years ago. It was before I married Count Harrisch."

"I thought so," he triumphantly said, proud of his recognition of her. "I loved your work in *The Blue Willow* and the *Mongoose*. I also saw you in *Lady Jane Gray*. The fear you emanated was classic, just wonderful."

"My, my, your flattery is building up my ego."

"You were wonderful."

"My, my," she said again. "But again that was so long ago it's not worth mentioning to anyone," she said, worried that the cat might be out of the bag. "I really would appreciate it if you wouldn't mention it to anyone, especially Betty. I, for some reason, don't want her to know. Please understand, I am not apologizing for doing film and theater work. I just don't think she needs to be bothered by it."

"All right. My lips are sealed," Kevin said, wondering.

"Thank you. It will be our little secret," she said, praying he wouldn't betray her. It was bad enough she had let it change her life, causing others' lives to change because of hers. Would this always be an albatross around her neck? Would it ever bring something good? She didn't know. Why did being in theater have such a bad connotation to it, especially for women? She hoped her good reputation now would overshadow her past, if it should arise.

"Countess Harrisch, I wonder if I could ask you to speak at school? You would make a very interesting speaker. Your story of going from America to Vienna and the life you led there—I think it would be inspirational for many of the students. You don't have to include your theater life if you don't want to."

"My goodness. Let me think about it for a little while. Again you flatter me," she said, looking at him.

"Every Thursday at afternoon assembly, someone comes in to speak."

"Thursday afternoons?"

"Yes."

"All right. I'd love to do it. To speak of my dear count and Vienna is my pleasure."

"Oh, thank you," Kevin said. She would be more than perfect, and he wouldn't tell Betty anything, word of honor.

Thursdays assembly came quicker than the countess imagined. She'd thought for a number of days what she would talk about and decided to speak of what the daily life of a countess was like—meetings, luncheons, visiting the poor and elderly, visiting hospitals and children's charities, representing the country, and judging various horse shows, flower shows, and agricultural events. All in all, it was an interesting behind-the-scenes subject, one most people knew nothing about.

Mary Ville, daughter of legendary Broadway producer Stuart Samual Ville and self-educated expert on old films and all the former stars, sat in the audience. She'd just arrived in time to get a good seat near the front, saving the seat beside her for Linda Allen, her daily partner in crime for disruption of evening study hall. They had a reputation that put a lot of gray in Stuart's hair. The more he lectured, scolded, and threatened her, the less good it did.

Mary was Mary and then some. Smart as a tack with long blonde hair and a turned-up nose over a pouty mouth, which told her widowed father all the news from school. She was incorrigible and her father idolized her. The countess's talk kept everyone interested with over twenty questions asked afterward. She still had stage presence and could hold an audience, Stuart Villa's daughter noticed.

"Countess, your speech was wonderful," Mary said, coming up and introducing herself and thanking her for speaking. "Did I see you in *The Starry Morning*? Do you do stage work? My father Stuart Villa is desperately looking for someone like you for his new play. Would you be interested in auditioning for a part? He needs a special actress and you'd be perfect," Mary finished, almost out of breath.

"I'm afraid I don't do that."

"You were so fabulous in the movie *The Blue Willow*. Please come to the audition tomorrow afternoon at two thirty at the theater downtown. Looking forward to you being there. I'll tell Father you're coming. He'll faint when he hears you will come. Must dash now. Thank you," Mary said, running out the door, leaving the countess with her mouth open.

My, my, the countess thought, *what next?*

Mary Villa had started to stir something in Helen's deep memory. She couldn't believe she had ever made any impact on the public all those years ago and that someone actually knew her work now and recognized her. Maybe she should do it again; maybe she still had something to offer other than speaking of the remembrances she had of the work she did for Austria. She saw she still loved being on stage. It was still fun to get someone's attention hold it. Doing theater again might possibly create lovely additional money for her charities.

The countess spent the night thinking about the audition offer. Did she want to or not? What was the play about? How long a run? Lastly, could she really do it? Memorization had never been a problem, but could she do something like that now? And what would Betty think? Finally she decided. Yes, she'd try.

At 2:15 she opened the theater door with butterflies dancing in her stomach, walked in, and asked for Mr. Villa as he came toward her, smiling at recognizing her.

"Miss Taylor, thank you for coming," he said. "I'm Stuart Villa. My daughter was so excited telling me about you. I must say I'm excited too."

"Thank you, Mr. Villa," Helen said, looking around the drab brick-walled theater. "Your daughter is certainly a bundle of energy. Very impressive."

"Thank you. I trust her."

"I feel very complimented and nervous. I haven't done an audition in years."

"You'll be fine," he said, handing her a few pages from the script. "I'd like for you to read the Madam Jones part. I'll give you a few minutes."

"All right." Helen took the papers, went over to a chair against the wall, sat down, and read it.

Stuart watched her, noticing the expression on her face as she read the lines. "Yes, she's got it." He watched the mannerisms she did as she read the lines. He'd found the right actress.

They spent the next hour and a half going over the lines, playing off each other, and building a former actress's trust and confidence.

"Helen, you're hired. Let me buy you a drink. I need one."

"Okay," she agreed.

The drink turned into two, which led Helen to share with Stuart her apprehension about being on stage again, but he wasn't worried and let her know all would be well, bringing her to come for the next week of intense and productive evening rehearsals.

Two days after the start of rehearsal, Helen called Betty.

"Betty, Countess Harrisch is on the phone," Mollie called to her.

"Hello, how are you?"

"I'm fine. I have, as of the other day, actually the day I met your friend Mary Villa, become involved with theater. I have been cast in a new play, *The White Bird*, produced by Stuart Villa."

"How exciting," Betty said, loving the idea of knowing someone other than Kevin in theater. The countess was full of surprises.

"I'd like to ask you to be my dresser for the show."

"Me?" Betty was speechless.

"Yes, you. You'll be perfect. It's not hard."

"I'd love to." Betty smiled at the phone.

"Thank you. I'll need you tomorrow and until the end of the play. I'll get a driver to pick you up about 6:00 p.m. to take us to the theater then back home after a light supper after the theater at my hotel, if you can stay that long."

"That's wonderful. I'd be happy to do it."

"I don't want to interfere in your life," Helen said, now hoping she hadn't overstepped the boundary.

"It will be fine," Betty assured her.

"Okay then it's set. Thank you again, sweet girl."

"You're welcome," Betty said. A unique feeling came over her. She'd never been called any special name by the countess before. It was very nice. She smiled. "Bye bye."

"Bye."

"Betty, what did the countess have to say," Mollie asked from the other room.

"Something very unusual." Betty was smiling, feeling very honored by the conversation.

"What?"

"She told me she was going to be in a play and wanted to know if I'd be her dresser," Betty said, going in to sit with her mother.

"That is unusual. I didn't know she was involved in theater. I'm very surprised, *shocked* is the real word," Mollie said, looking at Betty with an underthought that all actresses are loose women.

"Me too. I don't think I'm shocked, but I am definitely surprised."

"Why didn't we know she is an actress?"

"I guess she never mentioned it. It must not have been a big part of her life."

"She just doesn't seem the type. I don't know if I approve of you being her dresser. Actresses and all that. It isn't the company I would choose for you." Mollie's old-fashioned ideas came to the surface.

"Mother, that's silly. You and I know her as she is, the countess, not the actress. Anyway she will only be doing this one play, and she was asked to do it by Stuart Ville."

"Who is Stuart Ville?" Mollie asked.

"Mother! How is it that you don't know that name?"

"I really don't know."

"He's a well-known Broadway producer."

"Oh," Mollie said flatly.

"His daughter is in school with me."

"Oh," again came from Mollie. "I'm beginning to wonder who our countess is."

"Our countess, as you put it, is a somewhat sad lady who has lost her husband. She is here to raise monies for her charities, and she is a nice person," Betty said, not believing her mother's attitude.

"That's true. All right. I must admit I like her, but I am surprised," Mollie told Betty as she wondered how an actress becomes a countess.

"She said she'd pick me up about six. The driver would take us to the theater, then after, she invited me for a light supper."

"That is very generous of her. When is this play?"

"It starts next weekend and runs for several days. She wants me there for dress rehearsals too, which are next week."

"What's it called and what's it about?" Mollie continued to ask.

"It's called The *White Bird*, but I don't know what it's about," Betty said, also wondering about the play, adding, "This came about through my friend Mary Ville."

"Did I ever meet Mary?" Mollie asked.

"I don't think so. I like her, she's lots of fun," Betty said, smiling.

Chapter 25

At 6:00 p.m. a black car pulled up at the Careys' house to collect Betty. As Betty opened the door to go out, she could see the countess sitting in the backseat.

"Hello. Are you ready to be my dresser?" Helen asked, looking at Betty in the early evening light, still seeing Goff in her.

"I am. This should be fun. What do you want me to do?"

"The main thing is to be very ready to help me out of one costume and into another. It can be very quick, so you have to pay attention to what is said on stage. This show has only one tricky scene when I come off and everything must be ready for the change. It has to be done within about two minutes. You can't let me forget the shoes and the hat."

"I'll do my best."

"I'm sure we'll be fine. Timing and speed are everything."

"Okay."

"Tonight I want you to sit out front and listen to the director's instructions. There are a few scenes when you must be on either the right or left side of the stage. You'll see how and when I have to exit and enter," the actress told her not as a friend but as a professional, expecting perfection. Helen was surprised at herself. Her tone of voice seemed to change.

Was this play all that important? The answer was yes. For the last time it would bring her back to her beloved chosen life. Now Betty would also be a special part of things. She smiled inside, thinking her own daughter would be the one to help in opening a former door. She reached over, giving Betty's hand a little squeeze. Betty looked over at Helen. They smiled. She could tell the countess trusted her.

The lights dimmed. The audience settled down as the curtain slowly rose, exposing a living room on stage right and a large porch with a railing on stage left. A nervous countess, Helen Taylor, entered downstage. She came onto the porch and entered the living room carrying the mail. She proceeded to look through it, becoming excited by one of the letters. So began act 1, scene 1 of *The White Bird*, her last starring performance before official retirement.

She'd loved working in all the films she had done, but being onstage was her passion, and now years later she was back. All the years of theater and film had brought her money and fame and very little time for the past, but there were times she caught herself having some kind of regretful thoughts but always dismissing them.

She absolutely had no time for it. Life went forward; that's all there was. This time she was doing it for fun.

As the curtain went down the applause thundered through the theater. She realized they really had remembered her from all those years ago. She stepped forward for a single bow and then stepped back and stepped forward again with the rest of the cast.

The crowd wouldn't let her go. Finally surrendering after a three-minute standing ovation, things settled down. The cast could barely leave the stage with all the flowers that were thrown on it as tribute. It was an expensive, beautiful mess.

"I'm so proud of you! They loved you," Betty said as Helen went backstage to the small dressing room to change.

"Thank you. This evening has made me very happy and somewhat sad. Betty, would you get the cards and some of the flowers, please?"

"Okay, but first let me help you out of that costume. We need to get it back to Ann in wardrobe," she said as she felt how warm Helen was.

"Do you think it looked good to the audience?" Helen asked, always a little fearful if things were good.

"Yes, very much so," Betty said.

Helen felt a bit sorry the first night was over. It had been great fun, and she had also shown herself and those that remembered that she could still do it, but the best part was that Betty, her Betty, had been her dresser and shared intimate moments as only an actress and dresser can. She sat down at the small dressing table, opened up a jar of cold cream, and applied it to her face, taking away the character she had just played. Betty gathered up the costumes, shoes, hats, and gloves that went into the show and took them over to Ann, gathering the cards, messages, and some of the flowers upon her return to the dressing room.

Wiping the last bit of cold cream off, Helen had a special sense of pride. An old happiness had returned. Opening night had been a success. A greater one than she had imagined. She never thought she would be onstage again or how her comeback would be so welcomed. Artistic vanity had ruled her earlier life, but tonight she took it all in stride, not wanting it to rule her life again. This was just a passing fancy.

Stuart Ville has preordered dinner and champagne to be served at the restaurant. He liked this restaurant for its forest feeling. Well-painted murals of big old oak trees with pheasants, grosse, and an elegant white owl that looked out at the diners, gave the room a very outdoorsy feeling. They offered a good solid menu of broiled steaks and various chops, potatoes cooked in several ways, and five kinds of pie for dessert.

Helen was seated at the head of a large table with Stuart on her left and Betty on her right and the rest of the cast and crew around. The conversation was directed to the show with Stuart telling the cast how pleased he was, but there were a few things that needed to be corrected. Helen came in too quickly in scene 4, John needed to speak softer in the love scene, and the lighting was too subtle. He couldn't see them well enough, and there was some noise from backstage, but in general he was pleased.

Betty sat there watching as Helen, not so modestly, enjoyed the evening. She had several glasses of champagne and heartily ate a big slice of roast beef with mashed potatoes. She later stood up to tell everyone how happy she was to be in this play. To be directed by Stuart was one of the best acting gigs she had, and she was very grateful for Betty's help.

While Betty watched, she was proud of Helen. This last statement made her feel closer to her than ever. They had become a theater team and without much effort. Often they were on the same thought wave, which both took for granted, but now Betty felt there was something more. She didn't understand it but realized they had a true connection. It wasn't just about working well together, but something deeper—more than the fact they had the same eye color and hair color, each with a silly cowlick on the left side of their scalp, or that each liked lima beans and tomatoes but didn't like sauerkraut. Betty liked Helen, not because she was an actress or a countess. She wanted to spend time with her, to get to know her. This connection was growing. It was interesting to find friendship with an older woman.

The evening lasted until almost 1:00 a.m. As Helen and Betty got in the car, again she told her she couldn't have done it without her wonderful help.

Mollie was waiting up as Betty came in the front door.

"Hello, my sweet girl," Mollie greeted her daughter.

"Hello, Mother. I had a great evening. The play was wonderful, and the audience gave Helen a standing ovation."

"My goodness. I'm sorry I wasn't there."

"After, we all went out for dinner. It was a fantastic place. It looked like a forest."

"How fun."

"It was. But I was surprised at the big dinner Helen ate. She explained that acting made her very hungry. She drank three glasses of champagne."

"My, my. I bet you're tired, my sweet girl."

"I am. I'm going to bed. I'll tell you more about it tomorrow."

"Okay, darling," Mollie said, kissing Betty good night.

Betty literally flopped into bed. It was a good tired, brought on by a very full day.

As Betty flopped into bed, Helen went to hers with happy thoughts of the evening's success. As sleep came, not only were there thoughts of the evening but a twinge of her past also floated around in her head. Why had she given up Betty? Why, why?

"Public, glory, fame. I am so stupid. How much did I lose because of it? I had the count, but he was all. Betty. Tonight. Roast beef." Sleep came, bringing a darkness with dreams of her early days of selfish desire, muddling the night.

She woke up tired. Tonight would be another show. She had forgotten how much energy it took to do a show and how much her nerves were affected, but she had no regrets. It was the right thing. She was in her element. And the party. Never had she enjoyed an after-theater party like that. Had she really eaten all that roast beef and potatoes? Maybe it was the several glasses of champagne that brought the difficult night.

The next day was spent going over her lines and dealing with the stage fright she'd always had. These days it was the same. Someone had once told her it created a better performance. Did it?

Betty and Helen were at the theater right on time for the last performance of the show. Her nerves were more pronounced than ever. It worried Betty.

"Betty, don't worry. This happens all the time before a show. I've just been able to hide it until tonight. I've been away so long I'd forgotten the power of stage fright. They say it makes for a better show," Helen tried to explain.

"I'm sorry you go through this pacing and fear."

"Thank you, sweet girl, for your concern. I'll be fine." And she was the moment she stepped onto the stage.

The play was a success, and this portion of her return to the past told her the stage door was now closed. Somehow she didn't need it anymore. There were now more important things to be dealt with. Her guilty feelings of betrayal of Goff and Betty still ached deep in her heart. How she had been able to push them aside for all those years she didn't know.

Chapter 26

Helen invited Betty and Mollie to lunch soon after the play closed. That morning around 9:00 a.m., Mollie felt a slight headache coming. By ten it was worse and by eleven she was in bed with the drapes drawn.

"Betty, I don't feel well enough to go to lunch at the countess's."

"Mother, I'm sorry you feel so bad. Are you sure you don't need me to stay with you?"

"No, I just need quiet. I'll be fine by the time you get back. Could you please get me a couple of aspirins?"

"Okay," Betty said, bringing them to her a moment later.

"Thank you, dear. Please give the countess my regards. I have a small hostess gift for her on the kitchen table."

"I'll take it."

"Thank you," Mollie said, mentally cursing the pain.

As Betty drove out of the driveway, Mollie took the two aspirins. She snuggled into bed. It was a wonderful bed, and she liked being there.

Surely this thing will be gone by the time Betty gets back, she thought. She closed her eyes, trying to rest and relax.

Chapter 27

The weather that day was cloudy. A definite storm was brewing off to the west. It took about fifteen minutes for Betty to drive to Helen's.

Helen's heart beat faster while waiting for Betty to arrive. She felt nervous, as if she were going on some kind of first date.

I hope I have everything ready. Soup is on the stove, sandwiches on the counter, and the teapot is ready to make a nice brew. Yes. All set, she thought.

The doorbell rang. Helen straightened her dress and smoothed her hair as she got up to answer.

"Welcome, Betty. I'm so glad you could come. Where is your mother?"

"She isn't feeling well. She has a bad headache."

"Oh, I'm so sorry. Nothing worse than a headache," Helen sympathized.

"I agree. I sometimes have migraines," Betty told her.

"I know how terrible they can be. I also have them, but not for a long time," Helen said, remembering the nausea she used to feel, only wanting to be in a dark and quiet place.

"I'm sorry you also suffer them."

"Me too. But on a cheerier note, I hope you're hungry."

"Yes, I am," Betty said, handing Helen the small package Mollie had prepared.

"Oh, Betty, what is this?"

"Just a little something in appreciation for being invited."

"It is I who appreciate you being able to come," Helen said, opening the package and finding a lovely silk scarf, adding, "Betty, this is beautiful."

"I'm glad you like it."

"I do, I do. Come, let's go eat," Helen said, guiding Betty to the table.

Next Helen brought out, on a lovely tray, two big bowls of vegetable soup. The steaming broth gave off a wonderful, satisfying smell of something very homey. She put one in front of Betty and the other in front of her place as she sat down.

"This looks so good," Betty said, smiling at the hostess.

"I hope it will be. Would you like a sandwich? I've made sliced chicken and tomato," she said, offering a large plate of sandwich triangles.

"Please. They are beautiful."

"Thank you. I'm really not much of a cook, but I can make a nice sandwich."

"I would say so," Betty said, taking a bite. She sipped the soup. It was good.

"So tell me. What's new? How is school?"

"School is fine."

"Good. How is Kevin?" Helen calmly asked.

"Kevin is fine too."

"I'm glad. He seems like such a fine young man. Do give him my regards. How is your book coming along?"

"It keeps me thinking. I think I have a good plot idea."

"That's all it takes," Helen said.

"That's for sure."

"I find it most amazing that you write. I wonder where such talent comes from," she said. A moment later she worried if Betty would find this statement questionable.

"I don't know. It just seems to be there," Betty answered, wondering why the countess would wonder where her writing comes from.

"Does Kevin really want to become a professional actor? It is a difficult life."

"He really does. He just seems to know how to be on the stage. I'm proud to be with him."

"Don't be too proud too quickly," Helen said. "You need other boyfriends, not just one. There are many fish in the sea."

"I know, but Kevin has my heart."

"My girl, you have lots of time. Don't rush into anything too fast."

"You sound motherly."

"I care about you and your life. What does your mother say about him?"

"Well, the main problem with her is that he is Catholic and Irish. Granted, Daddy was Irish, but Mother didn't mind. She is, for some strange reason, afraid of Kevin."

"She is worried he will change you and take you away."

"But he won't."

"I hope not. Would you like some dessert? I have some lovely chocolate ice cream," Helen said, changing the subject.

"I'd love that," Betty agreed, letting the subject go.

"I love chocolate. It's like Sunday. Something special. One day it will be ordinary, I suppose."

"That might be, but I will always love it," Betty said, helping Helen take the dishes to the kitchen and putting them in her small sink. She watched as Helen dished up the ice cream. She liked watching Helen. There was something unique about her, but Betty didn't know what it was. She thought about it. She was pretty to look at but not beautiful. She had a very pretty dress and modern shoes, not those huge shoes some older women wore. She looked like a lady who knew something.

"I remember my aunt would sometimes invite us for lunch on Sunday. She was a nice lady, but she always served the same thing to us."

"What was it?" Betty asked.

"A strange combination, I thought. Roast duck with olives served over noodles."

"That's funny. Did you like it?"

"Not very much, but I ate it," she said, smiling at the remembrance.

"My mother likes French food, so she has our cook make all kinds of wonderful things," Betty said, smiling and remembering the kitchen of 2530 West Lake of the Isles Boulevard.

"I'm afraid I never had the time to learn to cook, and there was never a demand on me about it. Count Harrisch liked the native dishes of Hungary, so I did learn to make good Wiener schnitzel. I'll have to make it for you one day."

"I've never had it. I'd like that," Betty said.

"Okay, we'll have a schnitzel day."

"Tell me about your childhood. Where were you born? Who were your parents? Do you have any brothers and sisters?" Betty couldn't wait to know.

"My childhood was ordinary, nothing special. I was born in Stillwater, Minnesota. I had two brothers and a sister. My father worked as a lawyer. We had a big house and always had lots of pets. I loved theater and seemed to have a knack for acting."

"Tell me about your brothers and sister."

"They were nice people but much older than I am. Ed is ten years older. He worked on the railroad. He married a nice girl named Nancy. My other brother, Dustin, was a lawyer. He died several years ago. His family lives in Kansas. He was twelve years older, and my sister Elizabeth is a knitter. She is unmarried and lives in Madison, Wisconsin."

"Are you in touch with them?"

"Somewhat. Mainly at Christmas. I must say you remind me of Elizabeth a little bit. She is a smart and caring person, but sometimes I think she is too fussy. Being a knitter, she makes some of the most beautiful, complicated, and unique sweaters I've ever seen. I remember she knitted me a gorgeous shawl for my wedding. She used ribbon, not yarn." She paused for a moment as though the next thought shouldn't be shared, but it was. She continued, "I suppose I should tell you I was married and divorced before I married the count."

"Oh, my," Betty said, surprised by this confession. She'd never known anyone who had been divorced.

"It was my fault, but that's a story for another time. He is long gone."

"That's too bad," she said, wondering about how little is known of people.

"Yes, it is. Youth and stupidity seems to go hand in glove."

"Do you know what happened to him later?" Betty asked.

"He married again, worked for a laundry company in St. Paul, Minnesota, and is still there, I think. I haven't seen him in years."

"I don't know what to say."

"There isn't anything to say. It's all in the past," Helen told her in a cool voice.

"I guess that's right."

"The past is sometimes a very sad place, which drags people along in its wake, making them regret things that were done."

"What do you mean?"

"It is very hard for me to confess, but I trust you." She paused, looked down, and then again looked at Betty. She continued, "I had a sweet daughter with my first husband."

"What happened to her?"

"I gave her to my neighbor, not realizing she would give her to someone else," Helen said, now not being able to look at Betty. She began to lightly cry.

"How did that happen?"

"Back then there weren't laws about such things as there are today. My husband was off fighting in the war, so I thought I could temporarily give up my little girl. I went off to California to work, thinking my husband and I would get her back when he came home."

"What about her grandparents?"

"I could have given her to them, but because of our poor relationship I felt they wouldn't want her. They never approved of or liked me."

"I'm so sorry," Betty said, trying to comfort her.

"It turned out for the best, at least for my daughter. She was adopted by a wonderful family. They gave her a beautiful home, a happy childhood, and lots of wonderful love. She is now a successful young adult."

"That's good."

"Yes, it is."

"When my husband came back and found out I had gone to California and our child was missing, he divorced me."

"Oh, my."

"Betty, that is life, but I truly didn't realize it would happen. I blithely thought things would go back to normal. What is normal? I certainly didn't realize such a change would become the normal it has."

"So you got to be with your daughter again?"

"Yes, but only to know her from a distance."

"Does she know of you?" Betty continued.

"No."

"That's too bad. Maybe someday."

"I hope so," Helen said.

"I'm sorry you lost your child," Betty said.

"Well, as I said, I was too ambitious and selfish," Helen said. "I'm also very sorry. I don't want to think of this anymore. Let's go window shopping and for a cup of tea."

"All right."

Chapter 28

Helen got Betty back home at about seven that evening. It had been a hard day but a wonderful one because they were able to spend good time together. She wondered what Betty believed about what she told her. Did she really understand about the choices Helen made and the consequences of her actions? Was it too much?

That night, both went to bed wondering. In Helen's case, she was a little worried. She hadn't really confessed, just in general. What would Mollie think when Betty told her, if she told her. It was out of her hands.

The next morning Helen sat down to write Betty a note. She needed to tell her more details of what went on then. By the end of the day, she was exhausted. Confessing was hard; getting the words down so it made sense seemed to take forever. She would never again take writing for granted. With the last word written, she folded the letter, put it in a long white envelope, and wrote "Betty Carey" on the front. This was put beside Betty's poetry on the bookshelf in the living room to be discovered later.

Chapter 29

March that year came in like a lion—wind, snow, and sleet every day for two weeks. The year 1944 had already been tough with the war raging in Europe and Japan. Listening to the radio news every evening distressed Mollie. This constant hammering of so many killed every day, so many wounded, and the kinds of destruction done were heartbreaking. Mollie couldn't understand how there could be so much horridness. What had happened to the thinking of the world? Evil had always raised its ugly head, but this was insanity. In order to rid herself of the news, she would often take a nice, long, hot soaking bath. This began to become a habit. Seven in the evening became bath time. It was a good routine, gently putting her back into a proper sense of being. Sitting in the wonderful warm, lavender-scented water, Mollie easily let her mind think happy thoughts of Frank, Betty, her friends, and sometimes even a fleeting remembrance of her first boyfriend. Why him, she didn't know, but there he was.

One evening in early August, Betty had gone upstairs early to write a letter and go to bed. Mollie sat on the sunporch still enjoying the refreshing bath she stepped out of fifteen minutes before. The temperature had been in the nineties for most of the day. The evening had only brought the temperature down to eighty-five degrees.

Mollie opened the book she'd been reading but couldn't concentrate; it was too hot to think. Getting up to get a glass of cool water from the kitchen, she felt a strong pain in her chest. She had never had pain in her chest before. As the seconds turned into minutes, this strange pain intensified into a horrible stabbing. Her heart really hurt. She grabbed her chest as she tried to call for Betty but couldn't, as she fell back into the chair. God, it was bad; she couldn't move. The world seemed to go away like a fast-moving fog. She couldn't do a thing to stop it. Two minutes later she was dead.

Betty slept poorly that night. The heat and a strange restlessness kept her tossing and turning. By six that morning, the sunlight streamed into her room. Betty couldn't stand to be in bed another moment. The heat of the new day was beginning to plague everyone. It was already too hot to put on her robe, so she went to see Mollie without it. Not finding Mollie in her room and her bed made, Betty wondered where she was.

"Mother! You're up early. Where are you?"

No answer. She called again as she walked down the stairs, finally finding Mollie on the sunporch, slumped over in the chair. At first she thought her mother had fallen asleep down there, but she never did that. Going closer to wake her up, Betty touched her hand. She was cold. Even with the morning's heat she could feel Mollie's skin was cold. Betty realized Mollie was dead. The tears began to flow as panic set in and pushed aside her common sense of what to do—call the operator to get an ambulance. Yes, that was what was needed.

"Operator."

"Number, please." A solid-sounding voice came through the phone. "I think my mother is dead. I need an ambulance," Betty's weeping voice told her.

"Right away," she said.

"It's 2530 West Lake of the Isles Boulevard. Please come soon," she said between sobs.

"We're on our way."

"Good. Thank you," she said, putting the big black telephone receiver down into its cradle. She went back over to Mollie, knelt down, put her head on Mollie's lap, and sobbed bitterly. It was the kind of crying that ached. Her whole body was affected but mostly her tongue, throat, and eyes. The tears made Mollie's skirt wet. Slowly she began a quiet sobbing, calling out, "Why? Why? Why? Mother, Mother, Mother."

A few moments later the ambulance people were knocking at the door. Betty got up slowly, went over to let them in, and showed them where Mollie was. Things began to feel as though they were in slow motion. She could hear but not feel herself answering the questions the ambulance people had. She didn't know what she'd said, much less what the questions were. They put Mollie's body on a stretcher and covered it with a large white sheet, obscuring it from Betty's sight. Betty cried, letting her broken heart show itself.

The ambulance didn't drive fast or have its siren on. Betty followed behind, barely able to drive or see through her tears. "Death is such a wicked thief" kept going through her mind. It had been decided they would take Mollie to the funeral home.

Upon their arrival, Mollie's body was taken to the back for preparation, and Betty was greeted by Mr. Allen. He was a kind man, not forcing her into anything she didn't want. He showed her the caskets they offered. Betty looked them over, finally deciding on a light-beige one with golden handles. They also suggested various services or going to the family church for the funeral. Betty wanted things done in the church. She drove to the church they had attended for years, and as she walked into the nave, a terrible remembrance came. She could see her father's coffin there, and now her mother's would be there too.

Walking through the church, she found Reverend Smith's office. She knocked on the door. His secretary answered, letting her in.

"Is Reverend Smith available? I'm Betty Carey."

"Yes, he is," she said, knocking on the heavy brown door.

"Come in," Reverend Smith called from behind his desk.

"Hello, Reverend Smith. My mother Mollie Carey died this morning, and I would like to have her funeral here. Would you conduct the service?" Betty most humbly asked.

"Oh, Betty, I am so terribly sorry. I knew your mother very well. She was a nice lady," he said with a sense of welcome.

"What kind of service would you like?"

"I don't know. Something with the remembrance of her life and how others regarded her."

"That should be easy. When would you like the service? The church has very little going on this week."

"Maybe on Thursday. I would like a mid-to late-morning service, then have everyone come to the house for a light lunch."

"That sounds very nice. Do you want a few words said at the cemetery?"

"That would also be very nice. Yes," Betty said, starting to cry.

Reverend Smith handed her a handkerchief.

"Is there anything more I need to know or to do?"

"No, I don't think so."

Reverend Smith smiled. He had always liked and respected the Careys. "Now I have to write an obituary for her," Betty sighed. She thanked the reverend.

At that Betty got up to leave. A strong urge to see and be with the countess came. Half an hour later Betty rang Helen's doorbell. She started to cry again.

"Betty, what are all these tears? Have I done something wrong?" Helen asked, opening the door.

"Mother died this morning," she cried as Helen held out her arms, taking Betty in and holding her.

"I'm so sorry, darling. What happened? What can I do?"

"Just being here and opening the door to me. That's what I need," she said, feeling for the first time Helen's arms around her.

"Come in. Sit down. Now tell me," Helen said.

It was hard for Betty to get the story out. Helen listened, holding Betty's hand as she spoke.

"I'm in shock. Would you like to stay with me for a while?"

"I don't know what I want. Maybe you could help me compose an obituary for her."

"Of course. I'll help in any way you need. Let me make tea for us." Fifteen minutes later, Helen brought tea into her small dining room, poured it, and handed Betty a cup.

"We should take some notes. It should be fairly easy to compose." Two cups of Earl Grey tea later, the obituary was written.

"We need to get this to the newspaper. Maybe they can run it tomorrow morning," Helen suggested.

Later that afternoon Helen and Betty got the obituary to the newspaper. It would be in the paper on Tuesday and Wednesday. After the newspaper office, Helen took Betty back to her house.

"This is a beautiful house. Have you lived here your whole life?" Helen asked, looking around at the wonderful paintings, rugs, porcelain, and silver pieces that adorned the house. Helen was glad to see again the beauty of the house. It was exactly the sort of house she wanted for Betty. The only down part was that both Mr. and Mrs. Carey were deceased before Betty was twenty-five. All of a sudden she wondered if Betty had any interest in being on stage as she did, hoping for another link between them. Her friend Kevin did, but did Betty? If she did, it would be nice, but if she didn't then it didn't matter. She liked to write and seemed to be good at it. Helen was proud of her.

"Have you eaten anything today?" Helen asked.

"Not really," Betty answered, thinking she did not want to go out to eat.

"Can I make something for us? I'm not a very good cook, but I am good at figuring out how to eat leftovers or whatever is in the refrigerator."

"I'm not hungry," Betty said.

"I insist. Now let's go to the kitchen," Helen said, putting out her hand. Betty took it. They went to the kitchen and examined its possibilities. As they walked in, Helen noticed a loaf of white bread on the counter.

"Do you have some eggs and milk? I could make French toast."

"That's a nice idea. Eggs and milk are in the refrigerator. The pans are in the cupboard beside the stove. I'll get the plates and glasses," Betty said.

A moment later, Helen had the eggs and milk beaten together, the bread slices dipped in the mixture, and had it cooking in a large frying pan. She couldn't believe she was cooking for her daughter.

"I'll be your official French toast maker." Helen laughed.

"Sounds good. I accept." Betty laughed too. It seemed a bit strange she was laughing but stranger that Helen was cooking for her.

As Helen flipped the toast, Betty set the table, adding butter, jam, and maple syrup. She put herself at Mollie's place. When things were ready, they sat down, eating and talking. It felt terrible to Betty that Mollie wasn't with them. She was sorry, but Helen was there with her.

"Making French toast reminds me of my first husband," Helen said out of the blue. "He loved it."

Betty laughed. "Tell me about your first husband, if I may ask."

"We were crazy young kids. He was in the navy, and he was ordered overseas to help fight the war. He was a handsome man, tall, elegant, and fun. That's about all there is." Helen cut it short. "He's an elderly gentleman now."

"I'm glad you met and married the count," Betty said, wanting to, but afraid to get deeper into the countess's history.

"Do you think there will be a lot of people at the funeral?" Helen asked.

"I don't know, but I think so. She was well-liked. I'm sure many people will attend because they remember my father."

"I hope so," Helen genuinely said.

"I'm full. Thank you for feeding me," Betty told Helen.

"I don't feel like doing the dishes," Betty said. "Let's just put them in the sink. I'm tired. There's plenty of time for dishes later."

They got up from the table, went into the living room, and sat beside each other on the couch.

"Countess, would you mind if I went to bed?"

"Not at all. Rest. It will help," Helen told her. "I'll come back tomorrow." She watched Betty go upstairs and then went out the front door and drove back.

Finally Betty was alone. She went into her room, slowly undressed, and got into bed to think, mourn, and cry. What was her next step in life? Already she didn't like being alone. Just the word "alone" sounded so empty, but that's what she felt—alone. What next? What was she supposed to do now?

Chapter 30

The word had gotten out about Mollie's death before the obituary got into the newspaper. The next day was one of accepting food and sympathy calls brought by kind neighbors and friends. There seemed to be a never-ending parade. Betty was surprised and pleased at all the attention her mother got. She was also very pleased the countess came back to stay by her through this very hard time, giving Betty strength and a shoulder to cry on. That Thursday, Goff Leveroos stood about fifteenth in line at the church to give his condolences. He stood there looking at the people who'd come, all distinguished, mostly quiet, in their demeanor. He realized he wouldn't have much in common with any of them. This let his thoughts meander over to his team, the Minnesota Twins. *The bums. What have they been doing? Had they come to the point of waiting the opponent pitcher to hand them the runs? Why am I wasting my time on these bums?* his thoughts muttered. His next thoughts moved over to Mrs. Carey and to seeing Betty. He'd seen her on several occasions when he'd been delivering packages to people living in the West Lake of the Isles area, but that was ten years ago. Had he really been retired for ten years? Betty must be a beautiful woman by now. And now Helen came into his thoughts. He was still sorry they had parted, that she had left him and his family and had given Betty away, but he knew he wouldn't have done well as a father. Back then there was too much booze to be drunk and too many girls, but that was then. Now it is still nice to gently visit the Canadian Club bottle, but girls were out of the picture.

Granted he really liked and sometimes thought about Honey, as she was called, the salesgirl at Ramaley's Liquor Store; but she was just an old man's imaginary lust.

Yes, he was thinking he should pay his respects to Mrs. Carey, the woman who had taken care of his little girl.

When he arrived, he signed the guest book, giving his condolences and a few words of sympathy to Betty and her cousin Fred Johnson before he went into the sanctuary to get a seat on the aisle, not seeing Helen or she him.

The funeral was a solemn but beautiful remembrance of Mollie's life. Reverend Smith's words of encouragement and hope brought both pleasure and pain to Betty, who held Fred's hand through it all.

"Thank you for coming," Betty told Goff when he got up to her in the condolence line after the service. He smiled at her now, even sorrier than he'd been before she asked him if he would be coming to the club for some light refreshments. As she quickly spoke to him, she had a faint memory of this man, a quick flash from somewhere, maybe from her childhood. Was he really from her childhood? Funny how memories go.

"Thank you for including me," Goff said, touched by her generous soul. He still hadn't seen Helen, who had been there all along but now was in the powder room, nor had she seen him earlier. He walked away toward the door.

A few minutes later Helen returned, saying, "Betty, I think we should leave for the club now." She looked at Fred, who nodded in agreement.

"You're right. Let me ask Reverend Smith and his wife to join us there," Fred said.

Mrs. Malroy, Alice as she was called by Betty and Mollie, had made several of Mollie's favorite dishes, which were to be served. It was nothing less than what she knew Mrs. Carey would expect.

Betty and Fred arrived in time to greet the first friends. Helen was next, as was Reverend Smith and his wife Joanne, and nearly half of those expected.

Goff stayed back, not coming in right away. His conscience bothered him. Did he really have the right, and was he brave enough to attend a gathering of Mrs. Carey's friends and family after her funeral? Finally his curiosity and respect brought him up and in the front door.

The first to greet him was Betty, and then Fred. Coming up to give his condolences, he shook her hand. *This is a sad way to first meet my daughter. Gee she's pretty, like Helen was*, he thought, shaking her hand for the first time, feeling the touch of his daughter's hand in his. He smiled at her, wanting to spend some serious father-daughter time with her, if she would. His natural ease and charm led Betty to not care where or when she had seen him before. She liked him.

"Thank you for coming," Betty told him. This liking of him made her look deeper at him, wondering what it was about him that made her concentrate on him so strongly, other than he was a handsome man.

"This is my cousin, Fred Johnson. He's from Livingston, Montana."

"My condolences. It's nice to meet you. I'm Goff Leveroos," Goff said as he shook Fred's hand, noticing the roughness of Fred's skin and strong grip.

"Thank you. She was a nice lady," Fred said, adding, "I always loved being with them."

"You're from Montana. Such a beautiful place. I've always had an interest in the West," Goff said.

"It is beautiful. How is it you knew Aunt Mollie?" Fred asked as the next couple in line came to talk to Betty.

"I met her husband on several occasions," he said, crossing his fingers. "Oh." Fred smiled.

At that Goff turned to let several other people go ahead of him. As he turned, he thought he saw someone familiar out of the corner of his eye. He gasped. Was what he thought he saw real? Was it Helen, his Helen of so long ago? He looked away. He couldn't believe it; he looked again. Was his imagination playing tricks on him? He looked for a third time at her. Was it really her? How did she get here, and why was she here? He looked for a fourth time, this time seeing her turn full face. She didn't seem to notice, much less recognize him. He wondered, if they were to speak, what would he say to her or Betty or to anyone? Those moments showed him she hadn't changed much—some gray hair, a different hairstyle, but she still had the same womanliness he'd loved. Should he leave? he wondered but kept watching as she came up to Betty and stood beside her.

The minutes seemed to drag, as if in slow motion. As he got up the courage to go over to say hello, his fear put a nervous knot in his stomach. His brain raced as to what to say or expect from her.

Okay, now or never, and if it isn't, Helen so be it. I have to know, Goff thought.

It only took twenty steps to reach Betty and Helen, who were talking about the service and what a nice job Mrs. Malroy had done.

"Excuse me, ladies. It was a wonderful service," Goff offered, looking at Helen. She looked back.

"Are you Goff Leveroos?" Helen asked, now recognizing him and trying to hide her shock.

"Yes. Hello." He paused. "Do I know who you are?" he asked in the calmest voice he could muster up, his remembrance of her filling his mind as he looked at the older but still, to his thinking, beautiful woman.

"You might," Helen answered as her nerves riddled with guilt began to make her feel nauseous. Her hands began to sweat.

"I didn't know you two knew each other," Betty said, looking again at the handsome older man. "Excuse me, I see Mrs. Malroy is signaling me." Betty turned to see what Mrs. Malroy wanted.

"What are you doing here?" he asked with controlled anger in his voice that Helen recognized.

"I came to pay my respects."

"And how did you come to know Mrs. Carey?"

"I met her when I came back to Minneapolis. She was very kind to me," Helen answered, not looking at his face. She could hardly look at him and didn't want to see the look he had on his face.

"Oh, I think we need to talk. You have a lot of explaining to do," he said, again being calmed by her look, as in the past. She still seemed to have it, whatever it was, that was able to bring some understanding. He'd been putty in her hands, but he was stronger now and wasn't going to let her walk over him again.

"Yes, we need to talk," she agreed.

"Helen, let's go and sit over there, away from the noise," he said, pointing to a small love seat in the far corner of the room.

"I guess we have to," she quietly agreed, not wanting to.

Once seated, she looked at him. "I suppose you want to know what happened to me."

"Yes. How could you have left me and Betty? Why was there no word? What happened to Betty? I came home to find an empty home." His voice was almost crying.

"Goff, I can't talk about this in such a public place. I still have some pride," Helen said, looking down. She never dreamt this day would come. She'd so often wondered what she would say if the day came. Now here she was, unprepared. She wondered how angry he still was. What exactly did he want to know? How much of an apology was she to give? Would he forgive her? Was it too late? Had time done too much damage?

"All right, we're going to my place," Goff said. "I still live in St. Paul." Twenty minutes later, Goff put the key into the locked door of his apartment. He opened it, letting Helen in. He took her coat, putting it over a nearby chair, and offered her a drink. He wanted a drink to help him get through and maybe understand what he was about to hear. He made two short Canadian Club whiskeys with two ice cubes, handing one to her. As she took it, she looked up at him. He was still the good-looking man she had known twenty years ago, and he was still thin and elegant. Now for that second, she again asked herself why, why had she thrown everything away? She didn't know except for thinking the grass was greener on the other side.

"I don't know what to tell you, except I wanted to act. To be in theater and maybe in film. It's not a very good excuse, but that's what drove me."

"Did you care at all about Betty or me?" he asked, drinking his drink in one gulp.

"Yes, I did," she slowly said, handing her empty glass toward him. He took it, filling each of their glasses, giving a little more this time. "I care very much about Betty Gray. In fact I used to pass by the Carey house just to see if she was playing outside. Sometimes I saw her, but not very often. I also read of her equestrian achievements. She was often mentioned in the newspaper. I have a box full of clippings about her. She was something, winning cup after cup and ribbon after ribbon. So often I wanted to tell everyone, 'Look, my kid won on Saturday. Isn't she great!' What did you do after our divorce? By the way I found out about it when I got the divorce papers in the mail. I didn't deserve that, Helen."

"I'm sorry. You didn't deserve any of it," she agreed.

"I deserved Betty Gray. You're the one who didn't deserve her. You left her in the hands of strangers," he scolded. "Why did you throw our daughter away?"

"I didn't throw her away. I found out the best way to take care of her was to give her to Harriet Oates, who worked for the Careys. I didn't know Mrs. Carey would take her from Harriet. Betty was supposed to be with Mrs. Oates until I came back," Helen explained.

Goff listened. He didn't like hearing all of this, but he did listen. "All I did was go off and fight that damn war, and I came back to find both my wife and my child missing. It was unforgivable," Goff grouched as he took a long sip of his drink. He'd never been so angry and hurt, still not able to understand how she could do such a thing.

"I'm sorry. I really thought she'd be back with me after that film. Then there wouldn't have been anything to tell you. I had no intention of giving her up, much less letting her go for adoption."

"Did you ever talk to Harriet Oates while you were away? Through mail or telephone? And what about the Careys?"

"No."

"Why not?" he grouched again, looking at her face for some kind of clue to her thinking.

"I didn't think I needed to. I was satisfied where Betty was. I knew she was safe and would be fed and well taken care of with Mrs. Oates."

"What about what my thoughts were? And how well did you know this Mrs. Oates?"

"She was our neighbor across the hall. I thought you'd want her safe."

"Oh!" he grouched again. "I don't remember a Mrs. Oates."

"Yes. Goff, please stop. Betty was fine with Mrs. Oates, and she was far better off with the Careys, who could and did give her everything a child could need or want." Helen defended herself.

"Well, that's probably right. Mother didn't like you and probably wouldn't have made Betty happy. My sister Emily was off starting her art career, then marrying and having her own sons. This wouldn't have been a happy life for Betty. My other sister Ebba, she, let's say, really wasn't the motherly type."

"I know my mother-in-law didn't like me. I don't know why."

"She didn't approve of you being in theater. Sometimes her morals were too high," he said.

"How did we ever get to this point? We both lost the best thing about us, our little girl." Helen almost began to cry. She quickly took a long sip of her drink to hide her disappointment from him.

"Being young isn't all it's cracked up to be," he said, beginning to be sorry for her. "What happened to you?"

"In a nutshell, I got an offer to be in a film in Hollywood. I was cast as the second lead. Do you know how rare that is? I was over the moon, but Betty Gray, I had to take care of her. I didn't know what to do about her, so I asked Harriett Oates to take care of her while I was away. She agreed and I thought, okay. I'd earn proper money, someone was going to take care of my child—it was all good. Plus, my trip to California was paid for by the studio.

"Several days after we started the shoot, that's movie talk for filming, an Austrian count, Count Harrisch, came to visit the set. He asked me to dinner. As the days progressed I began to realize what a kind and generous man he was. We fell in love. When I told him of our divorce, he didn't care.

He just wanted me, actress, divorced—nothing seemed to matter. He was happy with me and all I brought along. I was so happy to marry him. We lived beautifully in Vienna until his death."

"How long ago was it?" Goff asked.

"Eight months ago."

"And now you're here trying to step in as though you haven't been away!" he grouched.

"Well, I didn't think of it quite like that. I wanted to know about Betty. I haven't been the totally distant mother you think. I always knew what was happening and where she was," Helen said defensively.

"I did too."

"So neither of us were bad parents," she said.

"Well, if that's true, why didn't I know where you were? I never heard of this Harrisch guy or where you were. You should have let me know where you and Betty were, and you should have known I cared," he repeated himself.

"We were divorced. I thought you wouldn't want to know of me."

"How could that be? I lost my child and my wife, and my home was gone. Things were so different when I got back. You took it all away. My world was gone," he almost shouted.

"I'm sorry, Goff. I'm now truly sorry," she quietly said, looking down at her glass.

"Me too," he answered more quietly.

"Isn't it interesting we're here together today?" she said.

"Amazing. Especially coming together at Mrs. Carey's funeral," he said, adding, "Why and how are you here? How much of all of this does Betty Gray know?"

"Nothing. She doesn't know anything about us," she said. "Who does she think you are?" he asked.

"She thinks I'm a friend of her mother's, and I am. We met at Strem's Fashion Studio one day a few years ago."

"This really puts things in question," he said.

"Yes, the question is should she know?" she answered, feeling unprepared about it.

"I don't know. I think we need to know each other first. I'd like to know her, but would she want to know us?" he asked.

"Maybe. What should we do?"

"That is the question of the century."

"For the moment, nothing."

"Right. But one day she should know."

"Probably, but not today. Mrs. Carey's death has been hard on her. She needs time," she told him.

"What about us?" he asked, not wanting to be her husband again.

"I don't know. There has been so much water under the bridge, our past hardly matters anymore."

"The past. Where's that? A lot of it I don't want to remember," he said in an almost confessional tone.

"I can't say the same."

Chapter 31

The service for Mollie was overwhelming; so many friends had come to say good-bye. Betty was touched by the honor given her mother by so many people, but it was hard for her, giving her so little time to think or feel what was needed. After everything was said, all the arrangements with the Minnetonka Club finished, and the friends gone home, she and Fred were back at Mollie's house. A horrid void crept into the Lake of the Isles house. This feeling created a loneliness that seemed to fill the big house. Both she and Fred felt it.

"Fred, I'm so tired. I'm glad it's over with," Betty said, sitting down on the couch.

"Me too. It was quite an event. There were some interesting people there. Who was that tall, good-looking man? I saw him leave with the countess," Fred asked.

"His name was Goff Leveroos. Funny I should remember that name. I only briefly said hello to him. I wonder why the countess would go off with him," Betty said.

"They seemed to be having a very intense talk. Did they know each other earlier?" he asked.

"That's a good question. I can only guess. We'll have to ask her tomorrow. I'm very surprised she went off with him without saying good-bye. So unlike her."

"That is strange," Fred said.

"I've become very fond of her. She's so nice."

"She is, isn't she?" he agreed.

"You know, I have a slight memory of someone like him from my childhood, but I can't place it."

"Memories can be tricky."

"I suppose so," she agreed, yawning. "I'm going up to bed now. Good night, Fred dear."

"Good night, Bets. Sleep well."

"You too."

Betty undressed, wanting to put the dress she'd worn that day in a special place. That dress needed preservation, and most likely she'd never wear it again. She got into bed; lying there, her mind went over the day. It had been full and equally as hard as the day she and her mother had buried her father. The new factor was the unfamiliar, good-looking Goff Leveroos. For some unexplained reason, he'd caught her attention. Who was he, and why had he shown up, she wondered. She supposed sometimes unknown people showed up at funerals. The thought was short as sleep took over.

The next morning she was awakened by Fred knocking at her door with a tray filled with buttered toast, jam, and a cup of tea.

"Morning, Bets," he greeted her.

"Fred. Morning. Oh, how kind of you. Thank you," she said, seeing him put the silver tray down on her dressing table.

"Can I pour you a cup of tea?" he asked.

"Please."

"What are we doing today?" he asked, watching as she sipped the tea.

"I don't have any plans. We need to rest."

"Good idea."

"But I do want to put my dress in the attic."

"Okay, you can do that. I'm going to bring in the newspaper," he said, turning toward the front door.

It only took a moment to finish her tea. Going to the attic, she found it to be the well-lit room she knew, due to the windows along the roof line, which brought in the light. Trying to get close to the hanging clothes pole, she had to pull out several large boxes. She put them behind her, hung the dress up, and put the first box back, looking down at the second one. On the cover she saw her father's handwritten label, "Betty Papers," in bold blue letters made from his fountain pen. She picked it up, taking it downstairs to examine.

My goodness, what is this? she wondered. "Fred, look what I found. Look at this box, look at the top. It's Daddy's handwriting." Betty showed him.

"I guess it is Uncle Frank's handwriting. Open it," he said.

"I'm afraid to," she said, touching the smooth paper on the box.

"Betty, don't be silly," he said.

Slowly she lifted the square cover, revealing a box filled with documents and newspaper articles. Taking part of them out, she put them on the small table near the door. They looked new, crisp, as though they had just been put there yesterday.

Taking the top document in her hand, she saw it was an adoption decree. What was this? Reading further, she saw her name. Was she adopted? Where, why, when? How could it be?

She'd never known she was adopted. Why didn't they tell her? She felt it must have been some kind of mistake. A quick read of the document clearly told her the adoptive parents Frank and Mollie Carey adopted the female child on March 17, 1917. Elizabeth Gray Leveroos, child of Godfrey and Helen Taylor Leveroos.

Betty couldn't believe it. She began to cry, almost wailing. The wailing noise scared Fred.

"Betty, Betty. What is it?" he asked.

Betty just held up the paper. He took the fancy document that stated, in beautifully scribed lettering, the adoption. After he read it, he continued, "Oh my, how could this be?" He was in disbelief.

"My birth parents aren't Mother and Daddy? I'm adopted?" She began to cry again. Large silvery tears fell from her eyes onto the document, blurring her vision.

"That can't be. I would've known, and this is the first I've ever heard of it," Fred said, looking at the papers and then going over to comfort her. "I've never heard anything, ever."

Her tears continued.

"Why didn't they tell me?" Betty sobbed. Her heart ached now.

"I don't know," he answered. "Let's see what else is there."

Slowly she stopped crying and then carefully looked at each document—feeling them, reading them out loud, not quite believing them, even though the unknown truth stared her in the face. Going through the stack, she found information she never knew. She began to realize it was true.

"If all this is true, who are my parents? Who are these people named Godfrey and Helen Leveroos written on the documents? Where are they? Why did they let me go?" she asked, looking straight at Fred, adding, "How did I get to Mother and Daddy?"

"That's too many questions. Maybe the answers are here. Let's look carefully," Fred said. He was almost more surprised than she was. His parents never said a word of Betty being adopted or her not being Uncle Frank and Aunt Mollie's daughter. Neither did anyone else.

Little was revealed as they looked and relooked over the papers. The information was old. From 1917, it was now 1940. They learned Godfrey Leveroos had lived in St. Paul. Betty assumed that Helen had lived there too. They also realized there was the possibility they were dead by now. It was now twenty-plus years later.

"I don't know what you can do, Betty," Fred gently said.

"I don't know either. I doubt any family friends would know, but I bet Daddy's business associates would know, but they are all dead by now."

"Maybe we don't need them. I just thought why not hire a detective?"

"That's an interesting idea. Okay. Where do you find one? Maybe in the phone book," she suggested, getting up to get the book. Turning to the *D* section, she found there were two detective agencies. Not knowing anything about either of them, she chose the one closest to the house. She hoped the McDonald's Modern Detective Agency would be able to find the Leverooses.

As she waited for the operator to connect them, she wondered what to tell them. A pleasant voice answered, asking how they can help.

"I would like to talk to someone about finding my family," Betty nervously answered.

"I'm sure we can help you, ma'am. Let me get Mr. McDonald on the line."

"Thank you," Betty said. Her hands began to sweat. Was she making a mistake? How hard was this going to be on her? Was it going to be expensive?

"Hello. George McDonald here. How can I help?" a deep serious voice answered.

"Mr. McDonald, my name is Betty Carey. I have recently been led to understand I was adopted. I would like you to find my birth parents," Betty coolly told him.

"I see. Could you come into my office to discuss this question?"

"I can. When would be a good time?"

"Tonight, about six."

"Six is good for me too. Where is your office?"

"It's on 587 Grand Avenue, second floor, number 283."

"Can I bring a friend?" she asked.

"Sure thing. Always a good idea." He sounded softer.

"Thank you. See you then," Betty said, smiling as she put the phone down. "Fred, we have an appointment at 6:00 p.m. tonight." Betty smiled. "I'm now a little afraid."

"Bets, don't be afraid. I'll go with you. It will be okay."

Arriving at the Grand Avenue address exactly on time, they found Mr. McDonald to be a middle-aged modern man with a pencil-shaped moustache, about six feet tall, gray eyes, and early graying hair. He looked like a detective.

"Come in, Miss Carey, and sit down," he said, looking at her, wondering how much trouble she was or she would bring him.

"This is my cousin Fred. As I mentioned on the phone I recently found out I was adopted, and I want you to find my family." She looked at his clothes. He didn't look cared for; he looked busy. She wondered.

"I'm not terribly busy now, so I have time to take you on. What can you tell me about them," he began, starting to take notes as Betty and Fred told him the story.

"All right. I'll start on it right away. Detective work can be slow, so don't expect results right away," he explained, lighting a cigarette. "Where can I contact you?"

"You can call me at home," she said, handing him her number.

"Good. We'll talk soon," he said almost pushing them out the door.

Going down the stairs, Fred said, "I think that went well, don't you?"

"I guess so. What am I going to do if he really finds them?" Betty asked, now becoming a little worried she'd taken the first step.

"I guess it depends on whether or not you want to meet them or have them in your life."

"Oh dear. I never thought about that or whether they want to be found or if they wanted me in their life."

"Maybe he won't find them."

"That would be very sad. I hope he does."

The next ten days Betty was very anxious. She was like a child, waiting for, but fearful of, Christmas. Fred was also worried. He was afraid her heart would be hurt if Mr. McDonald found them but they didn't want her. Finally late Saturday night, the phone rang. Betty answered.

"Miss Carey. I have found a Goff Leveroos. How do you want to handle it?" he asked. "Contacting someone can often be a tricky thing, depending on various things, like family circumstances, wife, children, et cetera, and what he thinks and how he feels about the past or what he's told his family."

"Oh dear, yes. I do want to contact him. I'm not giving up now," Betty told him. "What can you tell me?"

"So far I know he lives in St. Paul on Summit. He works for a dry cleaning company. He seems to be an ordinary man."

"What about Helen Leveroos?" Betty asked, now excited by the news.

"Haven't found anything on her. She seems to have disappeared about twenty years ago," he told her in a disinterested tone. "Some people just do that."

"That's too bad. Maybe she died," Betty said.

"That could be. I haven't found any evidence to that fact. Why don't I come by tomorrow morning to give you all my information?"

"Come around ten," Betty said.

"Sounds good. See you then."

"Fred, guess what? Mr. McDonald had found Godfrey Leveroos. He's coming in the morning to discuss the next step."

"That was quick. Good. I'm dying to know about him." Fred thought he didn't like Leveroos, yet he was very glad he'd given up Betty, his wonderful Bets. She'd always been his friend, his buddy, especially when his brother Evert had caused him so much trouble. Who took his side? Betty. Yes, it would be interesting to know this man's story.

"I don't quite know what to think. I love Mother and Daddy. They were the best, but if Mr. Leveroos and his wife hadn't given me to them, where would I be now? All kinds of questions are opening up. What will the answers be?" she asked Fred.

"Again, Bets, I don't know. I can hardly wonder what the questions are. I hope they will start to be answered tomorrow."

"Me too."

Chapter 32

Betty could hardly get things ready for Mr. McDonald's visit. She was excited yet nervous. At ten o'clock, the doorbell rang.

"Good morning, Mr. McDonald. Thank you for coming," Betty said as she led him into the living room where Fred also waited.

Before he sat down, Betty was given a large brown envelope. She took it over to the couch so Fred could see it too. Quickly opening it, she found a photo of Godfrey Leveroos. He wasn't, as Mr. McDonald had said, an ordinary man; on the contrary he was a very handsome man. Plus, he gave a report on where Goff Leveroos and his family lived, who all seemed to be in St. Paul.

She couldn't believe they had been so close all along. The mystery still stayed about Helen. Where and who was she?

"Oh, thank you, Mr. McDonald. This is all so interesting," Betty told him happily.

"Do you want to meet or make contact?"

"I think so, yes, as I said before."

"Okay. Now I have to contact him. This may take a few days again."

"Okay, do it."

"I'll let you know the result."

"Thank you. Would you like some coffee?"

"I'd love some, but I have to get in touch with Leveroos," the tall moustached man answered.

Later that morning, Mr. McDonald called the telephone number from the phone book. Godfrey Leveroos answered.

"I'm looking for Godfrey Leveroos. Is he there?"

"Speaking."

"Mr. Leveroos, I'm George McDonald, a detective employed by Miss Betty Carey. She's looking for her family."

Goff's heart began to race, as did his mind. His breathing became heavier from the understanding of this unexpected news. He grabbed for a cigarette and lit it.

"I believe you are her father," McDonald said.

Goff was stunned "She was given up for adoption back in 1918 by yourself and Helen Leveroos. Do you know of a Betty Carey?" he asked, realizing the bomb he'd put in the man's hands.

"I think I knew of a person named that. Is she looking for me?" Goff asked, feeling faint.

"If you are Godfrey Leveroos, then yes, she is."

"Oh my God! After all these years! How did she come to my name and where is she?"

"You are saying you are Godfrey Leveroos and you had a daughter named Betty, correct?"

"Yes."

"Well, Mr. Leveroos, she would like to have contact with you if you agree."

"Oh my goodness, little Betty Gray. Of course I agree. Where is she? I'd love to meet her."

Okay. I'll let her know. I'll call again to set up a place and time. Would that be all right?" Mr. McDonald asked.

"Yes. Oh my," Goff answered. "Thank you. You know I used to see her sometimes when she was little, playing outside. I never did anything about it because I didn't want to interrupt her life."

"I'll tell her you agree. Good-bye."

Goff sat there, taking several long drags on his cigarette. He couldn't believe it. Did Helen know? He wanted to tell her immediately.

Chapter 33

An hour later, Mr. McDonald had told Betty that Goff Leveroos was happy to hear about her and wanted to meet her. A plan to meet at Dayton's for coffee at 11:00 a.m. in two days was agreed to. They would recognize one another by the red carnations in their lapels.

That evening at home, Betty and Fred wondered what was next. "For the first time I'm afraid," she said. She felt as though she wanted to cry.

"Bets, I don't blame you. Who knows the whys of what happened earlier? What did those people go through that made them give you up? For sure it wasn't anything good. You'll have to listen to what he has to say."

"What can of worms have I started to open?" she asked. "Just give him a chance," Fred assured her.

"It's all I can do now. I'm beginning to think I need the countess. What would she tell me?" Betty said.

"No, you don't. She's a great friend, but this is a solo thing. I'm going to be nearby if you need me."

"I'm glad we've got each other."

Chapter 34

At 9:00 a.m. the next morning, Goff had Helen on the telephone. "Good morning. We have to discuss something. A detective hired by Betty Gray has contacted me. She is looking for her birth family. Apparently since Mrs. Carey's death, she has learned she's adopted, and she is looking for them," Goff told her.

Helen could hardly believe it. Her child was coming back.

"You'd better come here. You're right. We really need to talk," Helen said, beginning to feel flustered and a little afraid. "How will Betty feel since she already knows me as the countess? What would I tell her?" *I'll write her a letter explaining things*, she thought.

"I'll be there soon," he said. Goff was worried how he would explain why he allowed Betty to be with the Careys and why he didn't go after both Helen and Betty.

Helen was crying as she opened the door to Goff.

"Oh, baby, don't cry. The past has caught up with us. and now we have to pay the price," he said, coming in. He put his arms around her but quickly released her. She didn't want to be held.

"Goff, the baby days are long gone," she said, looking at him, not crying now. He looked very different to her—older, gray. A serious look about his face told her that life had not been that easy for him, but he was still a handsome man.

"I know. I'm sorry," he apologized.

"Good. Now what will we do about Betty Gray?"

"I'm not sure. I have a meeting with Betty at 11:00 a.m. day after tomorrow. I came to tell you about it and ask you to go with me."

"I'm not sure what to do. She already knows me as the countess. What do I say?"

"Maybe we don't have to say very much. We should see how she behaves and see what she says." He was also at a loss.

"Where is the meeting?"

"At Dayton's, and we are to have coffee. Remember she doesn't know we know each other."

"God, what a mess. Maybe we should arrive a little early so when she arrives she'll see both of us. It will be a great shock to her, especially to see me."

"It will be a shock for us too. Oh, and you should wear a red carnation so she will recognize us."

"Oh I'm beginning to worry. What if she rejects us?" she said, getting a lump in her throat.

"I don't think she will. She's the one looking for us."

"That's true. I'm going to write her a letter to try and explain things."

"A letter? Do you really think that is the best thing to do?"

"I don't know. At least I'll feel better about it. I think she needs a letter, some kind of explanation," Helen said, beginning to wonder how much she should tell.

"Maybe you should write something. When will you give it to her?"

"Maybe I won't have to," she said, starting to compose something in her head.

"That will depend on what we tell her."

"There's not much time before the meeting. I've got a thousand things to do. Meet me at the china department at ten thirty on Thursday."

"I'll be there. Sure hope Betty will really come," he said, adding, "I'm glad this is happening."

Chapter 35

The next day her mind raced as she wrote the letter. There were moments her heart beat so fast she thought she was having a heart attack. The really hard part was writing the letter. It took all her energy to put the confessional words down. Her nerves almost rattled to a point she couldn't sleep. The letter didn't come easily. Confessing was hard, and remembering was hard, but putting the words down on paper was the hardest. She'd only told the full truth to Heinrich; now she was trying to put it in a way as not to make herself look too bad. The bad, selfish mother, but that's what it was. She didn't want Betty to throw her away, to discard her. She began to pray the Lord would bring them together through forgiveness. "Please let Betty forgive me, please," she whispered over and over throughout the night.

The night was long and fast at the same time. Finally at around four, she dozed off, awakening around ten. "Oh my. I've got to get to Dayton's. Helen, get on the ball. Get the blue dress out, blue shoes, hat, and purse," she directed herself. "Now eat a piece of bread, put some butter on it. Quickly drink some juice."

She was amazed at how easily she got a cab. Maybe things were going to be all right on this gray, cloudy morning. Racing to the china department, she was so glad to see Goff already there with his red flower elegantly pinned to his lapel.

"Morning. Well, this is the big day. Where's your flower?"

"Morning. I've got it in my purse. Would you pin it on me, please?"

"Of course," he said, coming close to her. "I was so nervous during the night I must have smoked half a pack of cigarettes."

"My night was awful too. It took me a long time to write the letter to her, then I couldn't sleep."

"Sounds like we're singing the same song," he chuckled, trying not to let her see how nervous he was. "May I see the letter?" Goff looked around. "Look, there she is, the young woman wearing the red flower."

"I'm going to stand over there," Helen said, her fear mounting. "Too late to see the letter now."

"You're going to hide? Helen! She's your daughter too," he told her, almost like a father.

All of a sudden, a shyness came over her. She, for that moment, didn't want Betty to see her, or was it the countess she didn't want seen?

Betty also looked around searching for a red flower. Seeing one, she slowly walked toward the man wearing it. She started to somehow recognize him; at least she thought she saw something familiar. She wasn't sure what she saw in him. Did she know him? If she did, when and where?

He put out his right hand, saying, "Hello, Betty Gray. I'm very happy to see you. What a lovely woman you've become."

She took his hand. It was large, manly, and strong with long fingers and well-kept nails. He had beautiful white hair, well-combed, and he wore a nice gray suit. He seemed elegant. She bet he was smart. They held hands, it seemed to both, for a long time.

As Goff let go of her hand, he looked at her. He again saw Helen in her.

"We've met before, haven't we?" she asked, still wondering where they'd met.

"Yes. The last time I saw you was at Mrs. Carey's funeral."

"I think I remember. Yes, I do remember you. Thank you for coming to mother's funeral," she said, amazed his face had stuck with her from all those who had come to pay their respects.

"I wanted to see you and give you my sympathy," he said.

"Thank you. I didn't recognize you. I thought I knew all those who knew my parents. You remind me of a faraway remembrance I have of a tall man with a moustache, watching me play when I was little. I always thought he was Santa Claus checking up on me. Was it you?"

"It might have been. Sometimes I was able to go to Minneapolis, and I would come to West Lake of the Isles Boulevard. Sometimes I could see you playing outside. You were so fun to watch."

"That is so sweet," Betty said, almost feeling that had happened to someone else.

At that moment Betty saw Helen walking toward her wearing a red flower.

"What brings you here?" Betty asked, looking at the countess, not believing or understanding why she was wearing a red flower.

"Betty Gray. I am also a part of all of this," she said, not smiling. A look of sadness emanated from her eyes.

"How? You're Countess Harrisch. You can't be my mother."

"I'm Goff's former wife."

"What? This is so confusing," Betty said, her brain spinning from the new information. "Countess, I've known you for some time. You never said a word or indicated a thing."

"I couldn't. I couldn't destroy your relationship with Mrs. Carey. I wouldn't do such a thing. I was just so happy to be near you and to have you near me. Lord knows I wanted to be close, but it had to be from afar," she tried to explain.

"The same is true for me. That's why I didn't say anything to you when you were little and I watched you in your yard. The same was true at Mrs. Carey's funeral. What could I say?" Goff said, "Let's sit down. There's a table over there."

Betty was in shock. Mollie was her mother; now the countess is her mother. The handsome man from her childhood and at her mother's funeral is her father. How could that be? Slowly she walked with them to the table, sitting down from the one she knew as the countess and across from Goff.

"Betty, I know this is a big shock, but it's true. We don't want to hurt you or change you, but we think you deserve the truth. I'm sorry the Careys never told you that you were adopted. They were fine people and the perfect parents for you. We weren't. They were able to give you everything. It isn't that we didn't love you—we did—but life, the war, and stupidity got in the way," Helen told her.

"What does that mean?" Betty asked, looking straight at her. She began to feel cheated, betrayed. Deep down she knew Mollie would never have wanted her to know. She was a proud woman, and this wasn't a thing she could admit to. Betty began to see why she and Helen had so many things in common—same eye color, that silly cowlick, and both liked lima beans but not sauerkraut.

"Betty Gray, people didn't talk about such things back then. Nowadays they still don't."

"Mrs. Carey must have been very afraid of losing you. Afraid, perhaps, that you would leave them for us," Goff added.

"That's ridiculous! I love them. I'd never leave them," Betty said as a tear dropped gently unto her skirt.

"But that's human nature. The fear of rejection is a strong motif," Goff said, sipping his black coffee. He lit a cigarette, hoping it would take the edge off the conversation.

"I guess so," Betty agreed, still sniffing a little. Goff handed her his handkerchief.

"Thank you."

"Betty dear, don't cry. All we want now is to have another chance with you. We realize there has been a lot of time lost, but there is still a lot of time ahead in the future," Helen said as sweetly as she could, looking at Betty with asking eyes. She'd never seen Betty cry. It hurt.

Betty had heard the anxiety in their voices. She realized they had suffered, but she hadn't. It is amazing what the past can do and bring to the future.

Now Betty was sorry that Mollie and Frank were so afraid of losing her. She would always be their child regardless of blood. She believed Goff and the countess were basically good people, even though they'd let her go. She wanted to know what reasons they had for giving her up. What had happened?

"There were a number of reasons that pulled us apart. One was that Goff had to go fight in the war. Another was the sad fact that his mother, your grandmother, didn't like me because I was in theater, and lastly I left to do a film to earn money since my husband was away." Helen tried to explain, her nerves making her stomach hurt.

"Countess, tell me more about how I got to the Careys," Betty asked, looking straight at her.

"It was very simple. Your mother's housekeeper, Harriet Oates, knew Mr. and Mrs. Carey had recently lost a baby and desperately wanted a child. I gave you to Harriet to watch while I was in Hollywood. Due to things in Harriet's life, she knew she couldn't take proper care of you. She then told Mrs. Carey of the situation, who immediately went to get you."

"It sounds like the plot of a book," Betty said, amazed.

"It does, doesn't it? Maybe it will be one day," Helen said.

"It will be a long time until I understand everything," Betty answered, quietly adding, "Especially about the two of you. Everything is so fast."

"It's too much to tell you now, but in the meantime, I am so happy to be reunited with my child, my beautiful daughter," Helen told Betty.

Goff added, "Me too."

Betty smiled. She still liked the countess, as this is how she thought of her. Maybe the idea of being her mother would come later, but Mollie was her mother and the countess is the countess, her friend. She also liked Goff. He seemed so kind and nice. Fred still couldn't believe what was going on. As the meeting ended, both Goff and Helen couldn't believe how quickly Betty accepted them and the explanation they'd given about her life and theirs. There was much more to tell her about themselves, but this beginning was everything to Betty and them. The ties that bind were beginning to form.

Goff enjoyed being with Helen again, but he knew it was over between them. She wasn't the woman he'd married all those years ago. She had the same look but different—more mature with some gray hair and a few lines on her face, plus she was smarter, more confident. He didn't need to take care of her.

Helen also felt the difference in Goff's age. His graying hair and moustache were in a similar style, but he also had a look of maturity, as though he'd lived a somewhat hard life, which added to his good looks. He seemed calmer and surer of himself. He seemed to be his own man.

"It has been a very full day," Helen said, wanting to be alone, to absorb what she had just been through. "I think I want to go back. I need to rest."

"All right, we'll take you," Betty said.

"I'm glad we got things out. There is more to discuss," Goff said.

"Yes, later," Helen agreed, looking at him, feeling tired. She began to wonder if she should feel so tired. Granted everyone had been under a blitzkrieg of tension since the whole thing began.

When Betty got Helen back, she asked Betty to come the next morning for breakfast.

"I'll see you in the morning, darling. Around nine would be good."

"I'll be here. Sweet dreams."

"Thank you. Sweet dreams to you too," Helen said, pulling Betty close to her, kissing her on her cheek, and telling her she loved her.

Betty smiled, putting her arms around Helen in a long hug. Helen also hugged Fred.

Chapter 36

At 9:00 a.m. Betty rang Helen's doorbell. She answered right away, wearing a lovely yellow dress with long sleeves, an apron, and beige high heels. Her fatigue was gone.

"Come in, Betty dear. I've nearly got everything ready. Are you hungry?"

"Yes, I am."

"Good. Would you like to sit here in the dining room? I'll bring in some toast and eggs," Helen said, looking at Betty. She looked so young and fresh. She loved seeing her here.

"Let me help you," Betty said, also looking at Helen.

A moment later the food and tea were on the table.

"I can't believe I am so hungry this morning," Betty confessed. She usually didn't eat much breakfast, but this spread looked so appetizing. "Countess, everything is so good," Betty said, wiping her lips with her napkin.

"I hope you'll call me Mother one day," Helen said.

"I probably will. I want to."

"I'm glad. Are there any questions you want to ask me?" she asked, buttering another piece of toast.

"Well, I guess so. What became of you when I was little?" Betty boldly asked.

"I went to California and lived my life for art. When I learned that Europe had a lot of opportunities, I went there. I thought you were well taken care of with Harriet Oates, so I felt I was allowed to go. I planned on coming back, but things changed. Europe gave me a new perspective." Helen took a sip of her tea. She liked Earl Grey. It soothed her now in this stressful moment. Continuing, she said, "When you went to Harriet Oates, I gave her a package of your things. Among the things was a photo of you and me. It was the same one I had with me in California. I also included the cherub painting that had your birth name on it. I expected Harriet to keep all of this for you. I love that picture of us. You were so cute and such a good girl that day, I remember."

"I still don't understand how you could leave me," Betty said.

"I did it because I thought you would be better off. I didn't want your grandmother taking care of you. I needed to be in California."

Betty didn't know what to say next. She just sat there, mute, trying to put the pieces together. Why had this happened to her? What was she to do next? She immediately realized she wasn't to do anything. Everything had already been done. Now was the time to go in front of the past and to try to understand what had put her in this moment and how to deal with the new future.

"Betty dear, let's have another cup of tea."

Chapter 37

Several days later, Helen was feeling a tightness in her chest. It came on slowly, each day becoming a little stronger. Finally she went to her doctor, who put her in the hospital. They ran test after test, finally determining she was under too much stress. They said her life had to slow down, and she had to start living in a gentler way, or she would pay the consequences. She didn't want to hear that. Her life was just beginning to open up. She called Betty.

Chapter 38

"Countess, what has happened to you?" Betty asked as she entered Helen's hospital room carrying a big bouquet of flowers. She found a big jar, filled it with water, and put it on the dresser.

"Betty, darling, I'm so happy to see you. I think I'm feeling better already. Thank you for the beautiful flowers. The last person to bring me flowers like these was your father. He really was very romantic," Helen told her.

"Why are you here?" Betty asked.

"Oh, I don't know. Stress, they say."

"It must have been more than that," Betty drilled her.

"Now, Betty, wouldn't you rather hear about Goff? He was the most handsome man ever."

"Yes, I do want to hear about Goff. I'm really not sure what to call him or you," she said.

"Well, you will have to ask him. He probably wants to be called Dad," she said. "I'd be honored if you would call me Mother."

"All right. I'll have two mothers now."

"Betty, I've written you a letter. I've tried to explain what happened. I've got it here in my purse. She opened it, pulled out a fairly thick envelope, and handed it over to Betty.

"I hope you will understand when you read it. There's another thing I want you to think about. Kevin MacArthur. He is really a very fine young man."

"I think so too." Betty was very surprised by this advice and the letter. She sat down beside her mother, opening the sealed envelope, and she began to read.

December 15

Dear Betty,

How does one start a confession, or the asking for forgiveness or another chance? One just does it. It is not easy for me to tell you of the past, to change what you know, and maybe it's not fair, but I need to. I want you to know my side. My history.

As a young person I didn't know or understand what was important. I just lived my life not thinking of the future at all. I had strong ambitions and desires. I also had an almost restlessness about the theater, performing onstage. It was the only thing I didn't have to learn; it just seemed to be there. My curse was it drove me like an addiction, and I loved it and still do, even though the fire is just a remembering ember.

You know me as Countess Harrisch, wife of Count Heinrich Harrisch of Vienna, but before I was that, I lived in St. Paul. I lived there with my husband, Goff Leveroos, your birth father. In those days, people didn't approve of those in theater, but he didn't mind. But that wasn't the way Goff's family felt toward me.

I will never regret marrying him and that we had you. I had three passions then. My husband, you, and the theater, but the war took Goff away and left me with a very disagreeable mother-in-law, Sarah, and a baby. Sarah complained constantly about how I didn't take proper care of you and of me doing theater, which she said was only for cheap women. I couldn't stand her coldness and bickering at me, accusing me at every turn. It made my life miserable.

It wasn't as if I just left you off with Harriet Oates. I had gotten a chance to go to Hollywood to be in a film. Before I left, I didn't want your grandmother to take you. I told you all about it and that I would be back and we would be a family. I chose Harriet Oates to take care of you. I didn't know she couldn't. She's the one who brought you to the Careys, and they gave you a wonderful home, which I couldn't give you. I have no regrets about this part of it at all. My regret and sorrow is that I did it at all, that I wanted to be rich and famous, and I knew I could be. I am sorry I wasn't the mother I should have been because of my desire for money and fame, which took me away from my husband and home.

My talent and love of theater cursed me, not letting me give you the time and love you deserved. I had two choices, you and the theater, and foolishly I chose the second, thinking I would always be able to have you. This choice took me from the most important thing in any woman's life, her child. I've learned the hard way, done at your expense. I'm still trying to forgive myself. My heart has always been full of love for you, and I prayed you would forgive me. Now at the end of my life, I still have regrets, but since we've been together, my love for you is stronger than ever.

For years I have been trying to forgive myself, but I can't, and now I'm asking you to forgive me, to give me another chance. My life is empty at the thought of what I've done, but you have always been in my heart and prayers. That's the reason for the photo you saw in Marian Swan's house. That picture you and Kevin saw in the bedroom was a photo of who you thought it was, Countess Harrisch holding a baby. It is also a picture of Marian Swan holding a baby girl. I am and was Marian Swan. It is actually you and me. I keep a copy as a badge of honor, telling me I'd done something right. I've made some big mistakes in my life, but my long love for you isn't one of them. This photo is the only thing I had of you, so I put it in the bedroom of my Beverly Hills house to keep you near me. Back then film stars were not supposed to have children, so the story was formed that you were my niece.

I hope you can forgive me for my past sins. I love you.

Your birth mother.

It took Betty a few minutes to read Helen's letter. Her heart was broken by what those five people went through for her, but it all ended well, better than any novel, Betty thought.

THE END

www.ingramcontent.com/pod-product-compliance
Lightning Source LLC
Chambersburg PA
CBHW052026070526
44584CB00016B/1925